TWO BROTHERS TWO WARS

From the Western Front to the Burmese Jungle

THOMAS McALINDON

THE LILLIPUT PRESS
DUBLIN

First published 2008 by
The Lilliput Press
62–63 Sitric Road, Arbour Hill
Dublin 7, Ireland
www.lilliputpress.ie

ISBN 978 1 84351 145 8

1 3 5 7 9 10 8 6 4 2

Set in 13 pt on 16.3 pt Perpetua by Marsha Swan
Printed in England by MPG Books, Bodmin, Cornwall

CONTENTS

ACKNOWLEDGMENTS

In this recovery and imaginative reconstruction of the past I am much indebted to members of my own family, both living and dead. Two octogenerians with excellent memories, Albert Wilson and Henry McGeown, both of Derryinver, County Armagh, have been most helpful and patient in answering my enquiries. On military matters I am greatly indebted to James W. Taylor for his definitive study, *The 2nd Royal Irish Rifles* (2005), for lending me his copy of that battalion's War Diary and for his ready supply of information and advice on military history on many occasions. I am indebted also to the Irish Jesuit Archives for quotations from the unpublished War Reminiscences of Father Henry Gill. My researches in the archives of the Missionary Society of St Columban have been facilitated by the kindness and hospitality of the Columban Fathers, especially Fathers Pat Coughlan, Owen O'Leary, Michael Duffy and Neil Collins, all of whom conspired to make my visits to Donaghmede and Dalgan Park immensely pleasurable as well as fruitful.

I owe a special word of thanks to my old school friend, Alex Ashe, who in the 1990s drew my attention to a book long out of print, Francis Clifford's memoir *Desperate Journey* (1942); had he not done so, this book quite simply would never have been written. I have been most fortunate too in tracking down Clifford's son, Peter, and finding in him a generous source of information about his remarkable father. Finally, I must thank my editor, Fiona Dunne, whose sensitive and meticulous attention to detail has made my text much more acceptable than it would otherwise have been.

The quotation from Siegfried Sassoon's poem, 'Everyone Sang', appears by permission of the Estate of George Sassoon.

ABBREVIATIONS

Battn. Battalion

BEF British Expeditionary Force

CO Commanding Officer

Coy Company

CQMS Company Quarter Master Sergeant

DC District Commissioner

CSM Company Sergeant Major

DSO Distinguished Service Order

GOC General Officer Commanding

ICS Indian Civil Service

Lieut./Lt. Lieutenant

Lt. Col. Lieutenant Colonel

MC Military Cross

MG Machine Gun

MO Medical Officer

NCO Non-Commissioned Officer

OSS Office of Strategic Services

OC Officer Commanding

RAMC Royal Army Medical Corps

RFC Royal Flying Corps

RIR Royal Irish Rifles

'The pity of war, the pity war distilled.'
(Wilfrid Owen, 'Strange Meeting', 1918)

PREFACE

Captain Tom McAlindon, my namesake uncle, joined the British Army in 1908 at the age of seventeen, rose from the ranks and served with distinction on the Western Front from 1914 to 1918. A victim of the trenches, he was dead long before I was born. But although I never knew him personally, I learned much about him from my father and grandmother and other members of the family. As a boy, too, I would gaze intently on his portrait hanging in my grandmother's house and silently murmur his name, my name; he lived vividly in my imagination throughout my growing up. 'A boy's will is the wind's will,/And the thoughts of youth are long, long thoughts.'

The difficulties and disadvantages of a large family are many, but one of its benefits is that it can encompass a wide range of life histories that engage the interest of later generations of the family and promote a strong sense of life's manifold possibilities. Tom's youngest brother, Denis, his junior by seventeen years, was a pioneer missionary among Kachin tribesmen in the jungle-clad hills of northern Burma when in 1941 the Japanese invaded that country from the south-east and drove the British out with astonishing speed. Close to the borders of India and Tibet, his little mission station was so remote and difficult of access that he avoided discovery and internment by the Japanese and continued his work there until 1948.

I never made any connection between Denis's life history and Tom's, which was to me a thing apart: poignant and tragic, symbolic of the gigantic horror of the Western Front. I assumed that Denis did only the usual things a missionary would do — teach Christianity to the heathens, build schools and dispensaries. It was due to his unusual modesty and reticence, and perhaps insufficient curiosity on my part, that I failed to discover until very late that there was more than that to his Burmese days. Then in 1992 a memoir by a British army captain, written in 1944 and published posthumously in 1978, was drawn to my attention, and what I read there made me realize that there was a connection between Denis's career and Tom's: a haunting symmetrical unity in their two quite contrary histories. That realization prompted research in both the National Archives in London and the archives of the Columban Missionary Fathers in Dublin and Navan — and the writing of this two-part narrative.

PART ONE

World War I
The Western Front

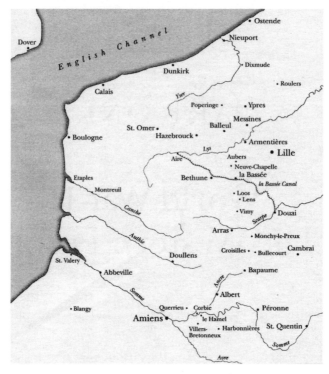

The Western Front, British Sector, 1914. Courtesy of Professor Richard Holmes.

The Ypres Salient, 1914. Courtesy of Professor Richard Holmes.

I

When Tom was an infant, his mother started work at 5 am every day in the loom shop of their cotter cottage in County Armagh. She would place the cradle as far from the rattling machine as she could, and tell his brother John, aged two, to rock the cradle when the baby cried. She told them about that when they were lads and it became the first paragraph in their mental history of themselves.

That was 1890 and Sarah was twenty-four at the time, having married Hugh McAlindon at the age of twenty-one. She was not the first or last sensible young woman to marry a feckless charmer, but it was as much the desire to escape from a harsh mother as Hugh's good looks and jovial manner that got her into this marriage. He was not made for marriage, it was said, even by his own family. He disappeared when she became pregnant with Edward, the third child, and for several years no one could locate him. He had joined one of the Irish regiments in the British army, quarrelled with his sergeant major, deserted, and prudently joined another Irish regiment; no better way, he thought, to escape detection by the military police. By chance, however, a young soldier in the same regiment and from the same area as himself casually mentioned him in a letter home. Enquiries were made by Sarah's father and it was discovered that he had signed himself as 'unattached' when enlisting; whereupon he was dishonourably discharged and sent back to his wife in County Armagh by an outraged battalion commander. Once home, he was cheerfully unapologetic and gave out that he was glad to be shot of the British army and back where he belonged.

In the census return of 1911 – four years before his death from cancer at the age of fifty-one – he put himself down as a weaver, as did Sarah. Domestic weaving in County Armagh during the nineteenth and early-twentieth centuries was largely a male occupation, but in fact all the weaving in this house was now done by Sarah, with help from the boys when they reached the age of ten or twelve. The father found a job more to his liking in a little pub in the Bannfoot (or Charlestown), two miles from his home in Derryloiste. He would wander home besotted on Saturday nights, having spent his wages in after-hours drinking with some bachelor cronies. He fathered four more children on Sarah, to whom the priest explained in the confessional that denying a husband his conjugal rights was a grave sin, that a large family was a blessing, and that the Lord would provide. 'Well,' she said drily to a granddaughter many years later, 'the Lord sure needed a helpin' hand.' Every Saturday she walked seven miles into Lurgan to deliver her finished weave to a middleman and collect the raw material for another week's work. But that was not all. With hammer and last, knife and leather, she repaired her own and the children's shoes, something she had learned from watching her father; she kept a cow and a hen run, a vegetable and fruit garden and an orchard; she baked bread, churned butter and made blackcurrant and rhubarb jam. When she was not exhausted, she told the children good stories; and she loved fireside craic when neighbours dropped in on Sunday night. She lived in the same house for the rest of her life, and during World War II, when the Germans bombed Belfast, she kept three of her grandchildren as evacuees. Almost two decades later, she cossetted one of them when he came in search of peace and quiet to work on his doctoral thesis for Cambridge University. She lived until she was ninety-one.

Derryloiste, and the adjacent townlands of Derrytrasna, Derryinver and Derryadd, are collectively known as The Montiaghs (pronounced 'Munchies'), which is Gaelic for 'bogland'. Located where the River Bann flows into Lough Neagh, the largest lake in Britain and Ireland, it is an unlovely place, flat and featureless; a place to escape from. Into this corner of the county the dispossessed natives of the surrounding agriculturally profitable areas were squeezed during the plantation and penal years of the seventeenth century. Such value as the place had lay in its turf, which provided firing for many homes in Lurgan town, as well as for the local inhabitants. The McAlindons' small holding consisted partly of reclaimed land and partly of bog or 'moss'. 'Moss' is the Old English (Anglo-Saxon) word for 'bog' or 'marsh', and although 'bog' is a word of Gaelic derivation, it was never used in Armagh, 'moss' being the preferred term; a linguistic sign, perhaps, of the complex historical relationships between the Irish and the English to which this narrative bears witness.

On their reclaimed land were a grazing field for the cow and a hay meadow for its winter fodder, as well as a vegetable garden, an orchard and a potato patch. But the moss was crucial to the family's survival, too. All the raised bog had been used up when Sarah and her husband got the place, so the kind of fuel they extracted from their acre of moss was known as 'mud turf'. This was obtained by digging a trench two to three yards wide and up to thirty yards long. In order to cope with flooding, it would be opened up in daily sections about six yards long, with a wall left between each; on the following morning, the previous day's section would have filled with water. Flammable mud would be found at a depth of three feet and would be taken down to a depth of about eight feet. Barefooted and with cut-off trousers, one man would shovel the mud up on to the bank, where someone else, similarly attired, would spread it out with a shovel and sieve out fire-lighter scraps of oak and ash with a four-pronged fork or 'graipe'. The mud was then formed by hand into brickettes, left to dry in the sun, later lifted for further drying and finally made up into a long narrow stack from which a wheelbarrow load would be collected every day for the rest of the year.

Tom and his brothers did the graiping and spreading from the age of ten and helped their maternal uncle with short spells underground when they were about fourteen. Plastered in mud and sweat, they would arrive home exhausted on summer evenings, and after two or three weeks' hard labour they would look with relief and satisfaction at the long, brimming trench or 'drain' that had yielded enough to keep the home fire burning for another year. Black and deep, however, these bog holes were a permanent danger to wandering children, and there were many warning tales of little ones who fell in and drowned. There was something sinister in their black stillness.

Thus close was the family to the elements of earth and water. Even in the reclaimed acres, if one dug a hole of two or three feet deep it would quickly fill with water. For someone like Tom, who would endure for almost four years the muddy trenches and the flooded shellholes and craters of Flanders, where many of his wounded and exhausted comrades would drown, to have grown up in the Montiaghs was a kind of apprenticeship. Or a prefigurement of destiny. 'Flanders', meaning 'marshland', is a synonym for 'Montiaghs'.

In those grim years in Belgium and France, the only things of beauty from the Montiaghs that Tom could summon as consolations to memory were the great metallic-blue dragonflies that hovered and skimmed on hot summer days over the glassy black surface of the old bogholes, and the butterflies that flitted about the heather and the blaeberry patches in the farther reaches of the moss – peacocks, small blues and dainty, darting coppers. The master in Derrytrasna school was an enthusiastic lepidopterist who opened his eyes to such things. What makes them so beautiful, what indeed is the chief source of beauty? he would ask. Bilateral symmetry, he would explain, perfect balance, every detail, pattern and colour on one side matched on the opposite side. And

then he would wander off into language and politics. Bilateral symmetry, he said, was a Roman word and a Greek word stuck together.
Did they know that we often talk Latin and Greek without realizing
it? Now there's history for you, an interesting mess. War and peace,
conflict and union, all mixed up; the Romans conquered the Greeks,
the Normans invaded England and the Anglo-Norman-English invaded
Ireland; my Irish mother's name is Fitzgibbon and she's descended from
one of them. The master was a great reader, everyone said; according
to the priest, his front room in Lurgan was stacked from floor to ceiling
with books. He would love to have gone to university, but for familiar
reasons that was a hopeless aspiration for all but a few Irish Catholics.
And for the likes of Tom, intelligent and resourceful though he was,
even a secondary education was out of the question. Survival on the
breadline was the family's one concern.

2

He left school when he was twelve, the minimum leaving age at the time. For two years he made himself useful at home, working on the loom, in the garden, the hayfield, the moss; and making 'champ' for dinner (a mixture of potatoes, butter, soft-boiled eggs and scallions) and pancakes, maybe, for tea, for he was 'a handy wee cook', his mother said. He also earned a few shillings for his mother working as an extra hand in times of special need on small farms nearby. But she did not discourage him when in 1904, at the age of fourteen, he decided to leave home. The family was growing and there were too many mouths to feed. John had settled in as a full-time domestic weaver (though he would eventually emigrate to Canada). They had three younger brothers and a sister still at school; there was a baby girl of two and another child on the way. Thanks to an advertisement spotted in *The Lurgan Mail* by the master, Tom found employment as a live-in labourer with a Mr Bruce of Holywood in County Down. Bruce found that the master's testimonial describing him as a conscientious, intelligent lad and no stranger to hard work, was correct.

For three years he served as an assistant to the elderly gardener and general factotum at the Bruce residence and would have succeeded him if the lure of adventure and foreign fields had not taken hold of him. A few miles from Holywood was the garrison town of Newtownards where on an afternoon off in 1908 he and a new-found friend, Billy C (as he always called him), gave willing ear to Sergeant Major O'Toole, recruiting officer for the Royal Irish Rifles (RIR). They were much impressed by his account of all that the army could offer. Tom's imagination had already been stirred in that direction, not by his father, whose allusions to the army were few and caustic, but by an old friend of his maternal uncle, a retired fusilier who told colourful yarns of his years in India and Burma; in Tom's bleak corner of Armagh, those names rang like magical incantations. But his practical, home-loving side and his sense of responsibility to his mother were attracted too by the assurance that the army could provide him with regular pay, a basic education and a trade to equip him for return to civilian life after seven years' service, should that be his choice.

When O'Toole asked their ages, Billy said he was eighteen, and Tom seventeen and a half. The sergeant explained that eighteen was the minimum age for enlistment to the Regulars, but that the problem could be solved: Tom could enlist in the reserves for six months and then transfer to the Regulars. They could do their basic training together with the new intake in Newtownards and if they were up to it they would be shipped off to England – and in due time to foreign fields, 'no doubt about that'. They were to think it over, talk to their parents and come back in a week or two, at the most. They gave it a week's thought and decided they would enlist. When Tom announced his intentions at home, his father curled his lip and said, 'The more fool you'; his mother was her usual stoical self, and his sister cried.

All weekend he dandled and played with baby Denis, the eighth child. On Monday morning he said goodbye to the family and at Derrytrasna crossroads called in at the school for a parting word with the master, the true father he never had. In the little porch, the master placed both hands on his shoulders and wished him Godspeed. When Tom crossed the schoolyard to the gate, he looked back and the master was still standing at the door, waving goodbye. Years later the master would recall how carefully he closed the gate behind him before stepping out on to Lurgan Road, the High Road as it was called then. In his mind at that moment, as in the minds of all youth looking to the years ahead, it would have seemed the beginning of a road that has no end.

3

Examined and passed fit by the medical officer on 5 February 1908, they signed their enlistment forms and were passed on to the quartermaster. This phlegmatic NCO equipped them with two pairs of everything – a great novelty for Tom, always waiting for John's cast-offs – and a black kitbag with their name and army number stencilled in white. Tom's number was 6062. Their numbers would follow them to the grave, and it marked the beginning of a process designed to turn them into impersonal objects, instruments in a great military machine. Thus they came next under the hand of the terrifying Sergeant Major McCracken and his pitiless corporals. If O'Toole's aim was to lure them into the army, the regime laid down by McCracken and his NCOs seemed designed to prove them unfit in every way and drive them back out again. What did poor Sergeant O'Toole know about boys and men? What ever came over him (they would ask) when he enlisted this lot?

Regimentation began with the trumpeter's 'Rouse' at dawn, and woe betide anyone who was a second late in responding. This was followed by washing and shaving in cold water and tin basins, the perfect prelude to a regime that made cleanliness and tidiness sacred virtues and developed all sorts of ingenious and perverse rituals to enforce them. Every piece of kit had to be folded and packed, and every bed in the barracks dressed, in the same particular way. Boots, belts, buckles, buttons, dummy cartridges, brass nameplates, fittings and screws: all had to be polished to a perfect glitter. Floors were scrubbed daily and at any other time the sergeant was dissatisfied with their appearance or was simply in a bad mood.

Drill was incessant, reflecting a frenzied determination to mould slack bodies into upright automata advancing and turning in perfect unison. There was endurance running in camp or down roads and lanes, until the weakest fainted and woke to suffer a barrage of acid scorn. Hours upon hours in the gymnasium, with press-ups by the hundred, stretch-exercises on the floor and the parallel bars, scrambling up seventy-feet ropes, vaulting over the wooden horse and over one another until the fittest reached the point of exhaustion. The townies among the recruits suffered terribly under this regime; country lads took to it more easily if unenthusiastically.

Punishment for any deviation from the correct procedure – real or imagined, blameworthy or not – was harsh and instantaneous: arriving a minute late for an unexpected parade, even after being caught short in 'the johns', meant an hour's run round the camp in full gear ('On the double, Slacker!'); a disarranged bed meant one hour scrubbing a spotless floor with carbolic soap; a slouching gait demanded impeccably upright marching in full kit round the square for the same period.

For some, the verbal assaults, compounding insult and sarcasm, were harder to take than the actual punishments. The NCOs had an arsenal of contemptuous names that poured forth with the speed of a Maxim gun; however hard they tried, the recruits were never at any time 'good lads' but almost always 'mammy's boys'; 'pathetic piglets'; 'whining wimps'; 'miserable arseholes'. The sergeant major thought he was cursed by God Almighty with the impossible task of turning them into men and soldiers, punished in this fate for some awful crime he never committed. What did he do, he thundered, to deserve them?

'Does he really mean it, the fuckin' bastard?' someone asked. 'He does and he doesn't,' said someone else. Tom thought it was a kind of game, carrot-and-stick (and told his brothers so). 'And where's the bloody carrot?' he was asked. 'It's the promise to make us what he calls men in spite of everything.' Billy C disagreed: 'It's making himself God Almighty and us nothing. He just loves to hear himself. I'll bet he practises it in front of the mirror.' They loathed him and found comfort in the comradeship of hatred.

He stunned them all on the morning of the last inspection parade. A stout, monocled colonel – the stereotype really did exist – went up and down the lines scrutinizing every third or fourth recruit with a careful but approving eye. In his farewell address he told them he thought they would be a credit to the 2nd Battalion, and Sergeant Major McCracken nodded and smiled his agreement. McCracken stood with them on the platform as they waited for the train from Donaghadee to take them to Belfast, all amiability, joking for the first time in six months. He wished them safe journey on the ferry to Liverpool and good luck in Aldershot, home of the British army. They didn't hate him any more. He really had been acting, they decided. In earnest, of course.

The 2nd Battalion had been back in England for four years after its stint in South Africa, so the expectation was that they would soon be off to one of the empire's faraway places, India or Burma or Indonesia. Instead they would spend the next six years training and practising sol-diership in various camps throughout the Home Counties of England: Hampshire, Wiltshire and Kent, with manoeuvres further afield in Cambridgeshire and Oxfordshire. The training was as fierce as ever. Rise at 5.30 am; a cup of cocoa and a biscuit, then a five-mile run; breakfast at eight and two hours with Sergeant Black, a tanned fitness fanatic from the army gymnastic staff, who worshipped the world's first great bodybuilder, Eugene Sandow; lunch and route-marching for twenty miles with 40 lbs of kit and stern instructions to sing and look happy when they passed through the villages; trenching and bayonet practice for hours every day. Manoeuvres, however, were strangely exciting: traversing vast stretches of the country, playing the great game of war, thinking of Wellington and Napoleon.

There was plenty of interest to write home about in the even hand-writing and plain, clear English that the master had often commended; his mother would read his letters to the whole family around the fire at night, leaving his two young sisters wide-eyed with wonder, glimpsing a much larger world than their own: a family ritual they all looked forward to. Everything was so different from the dark boglands, the drab towns and the dour city that were the limits of Tom's experience. The great rolling plateau of Salisbury Plain, blending earth and horizon and skies, seemed the antithesis of the Montiaghs; at its edge, there was Stone-henge, whose enigmatic magnificence, he intimated, eluded his powers of description. Towns like Salisbury and especially Amesbury, near Tid-worth camp, with its abbey in the park, its five-arched bridge over the Avon and its bustling, prosperous streets, he knew and liked most of all. But they encamped and trained too on the Kentish coast and enjoyed the attractions of Folkestone, Sandgate and Dover, developing then as seaside resorts, with bathing machines for the well-to-do, pleasure piers and even cinemas; there he was taught to swim, enjoyed ice creams at the pier cafés, and saw his first moving picture. A high point of 1910 was attendance at the king's funeral in London, when the Battalion lined the streets for the occasion and camped for two nights in Hyde Park. After breakfast in the park he saw the toffs and their grand ladies on horseback exuding all the arrogant elegance of an empire at play.

The taverns in Dover and Amesbury were a particular attraction for the riflemen and from time to time required the intervention of the hated Red Hats (the military police). He never mentioned these places in his letters and told no one but his brother Eddie about what happened in Amesbury in February 1909. They all had 'one too many' and some of them started quarrelling outside The George and fell to blows in Flower Lane, close to the premises of Mr H. Bishop, the town's undertaker. Tom was one of those who intervened to separate the antagonists, but they were all tarred with the same brush when the Red Hats brought them before Captain Wright, the company commander. Tom had been in the 2nd Battalion less than one year, and now a reprimand for drunkenness stood as a permanent blot on his conduct sheet. The shame of it burned deeply, not only because he had let himself down, but also because of his mother and the thought of what his father's drunkenness had done to her life. The like never happened again; his conduct sheet is otherwise flawless.

He redeemed himself in his own eyes and was proud to write home in May 1911 to report his promotion to the rank of lance corporal. He enclosed a snapshop of himself in a nicely ordered group of ten, 4–2–4, posed on rough ground against dense shrubbery; he stands with what looks like quiet pride, first on the right of the back row, his single stripe showing on his right arm. The others are all privates, aged, it would seem, between eighteen and twenty-one; they are his section, his men, and they, like him, are looking with cheerful innocence and boldly folded arms into a future that is beyond their imagining. Dog-eared and sepia-faded today, the picture tears at the heart the more one scrutinizes those eager young faces.

In 1912 he was made corporal. It was in that year, when billeted at Bhurpore Barracks in Tidworth, that he seems to have met up with an interesting new arrival, Rifleman John Lucy, a bright and loquacious eighteen-year-old from Cork, someone gifted not only with the gab but also with a literary talent that would flower many years later in a splendid memoir of life in the trenches, *There's a Devil in the Drum* (East Sussex: The Naval and Military Press 1938). Not having a secondary education (unlike Lucy), Tom took the third- and second- but did not attempt the first-class army certificate in education; that was for those who aspired to a commission; apart from the mockery that such an attempt would have won from his friends, Tom never thought of himself in that way, knowing instinctively that a Catholic labourer from the bogs of Armagh did not belong in an officers' mess. Because he thought it likely that he would return to civilian life after his seven-year stint, he took advantage in 1913 of the course in cookery offered by the army; his acknowledged excellence in musketry would be of no use in the outside world, but as a master cook he would not have to go back to labouring. He had already acquired the certificate in chiropody, reminding a sarcastic Billy C that an army marched on its feet as well as its stomach: a fact that carried much more significance than either of them imagined at the time.

Lance-Corporal McAlindon (back row, first right) with his section: Tidworth, c. 1910.

4

On being made sergeant in March 1914, however, he decided not to leave the army but signed up in June for another five years. It was a momentous decision. The 2nd Battalion was eagerly preparing for a transfer to Malta when in August of that year war with Germany was declared and they were shipped instead to France, as part of the British Expeditionary Force, bound for Belgium. To miss Malta was a great disappointment, yet the War was welcome in the ranks as among the officers. The long rehearsal of soldiership was coming to performance at last, there would be real action, and it had the flavour of justice and romance. Having bragged for years about their military strength, the invading Germans were to be driven out of Belgium, whose neutrality in the struggle between the great powers they were violating, and whose civilians they were treating with astounding brutality. On 22 August, the day before the Battle of Mons, when the British and German forces met for the first time, 384 Belgian males, aged between thirteen and eighty-four, were lined up against a church wall and shot dead in reprisal for the stiff resistance shown by Belgian soldiers to the invaders; and on the following day 618 men, women and children were shot in another act of reprisal. (That pragmatic self-interest – fears that an all-conquering Germany might pose a threat to the empire – had much to do with the British government's decision to go to war, is not a fact that filtered down to the fighting men.)

'Goodbye to all that': Amesbury, 1914. Courtesy of Mr Jim Fuller.

The British army, we have seen, was extremely well-trained, but as the Kaiser famously sneered, it was contemptibly small in comparison to the German one. Its men, however, were heroes to the French and the Belgians as they progressed by train and on foot from Rouen to Mons; in towns and villages they were cheered and kissed, garlanded with flowers and gifted with bottles of wine. The high point in this progress was on the afternoon of 20 August when the whole of the 7th Brigade, to which the 2nd Battalion belonged, did a route march from their billets in St Hilaire to the pretty village of Avesnes; here they were greeted with huge enthusiasm by the mayor, the curé and the entire population. Token gifts of the area's famous cheese were made to the officers. Nothing matches the anticipation of glorious triumph in a good cause for good people.

The encounter with the advancing German army sustained the illusion of glory for one day.

It was a warm and sunny morning [wrote Tom in his first letter home since landing in France — an excerpt found its way into The Irish News *of 28 November] and most of us were cheerily washing and drying our socks and shirts after that long hot tramp through France and Belgium when we got our orders to move. We marched past well-dressed churchgoers in Novelles as we made towards Harmignies in the vicinity of Mons. There we dug shallow trenches on a bluff outside the village and lay prone for four or five long hours under blue skies. It got hotter and hotter and we were tense and excited and a bit nervous, not knowing what to expect.*

Then at 3.45 pm the Germans began a prolonged and deafening barrage of high-explosive and shrapnel shells, most of which fell well behind the entrenched riflemen; when the barrage ceased, and it was assumed by the enemy that most of the defenders were dead, their grey-clad infantry emerged to attack in massed columns. Bunched together like this, they were easy targets for the British, whose rapid firing – twenty-five bullets per minute ('the mad minute' as it was called) – was so lethal that the German commanders reported that the British were relying mainly on machine guns, when in fact the Battalion actually had only two. Line after line of the massed enemy were reduced to crumpled and twitching bodies, yet still they kept coming on. 'The German commanders don't seem to mind how many of their men are killed,' Tom wrote (little imagining that the same would soon be said of the British commanders). When the Germans retreated, and then attacked and retreated a second time, it seemed like total victory; and indeed the losses on the German side in the battle as a whole were more than three times those of the British regiments (5000 as against 1600). As they surveyed the ground before them, littered with grey heaps that had been eager young men in the morning, the riflemen of the 2nd Battalion were at once horrified and elated, sensing an assurance of final success, the War over by Christmas as commonly predicted. Thus like all the other regiments involved in the day's battle, they were bewildered and shocked when they were told that instead of following up this victory they had to retreat promptly. As they would learn in due time, the BEF was being cut off from its French ally and was in danger of being outflanked by the numerically superior and better equipped German army.

The terrible reality of a war he could so easily have avoided (for conscription was never introduced in Ireland) came home to Tom in a singularly personal manner late on that first Sunday night. He was helping to carry the wounded to an improvised clearing station behind the trenches when he spotted on a bloodstained stretcher the body of an old friend, Corporal Pat Sharkey. His eyes were open, and there was a look of astonishment still on his face; a shell fragment had cut deep into his heart, killing him almost instantly. Tom and two others buried him in a shallow grave at dusk while bullets whistled dangerously about and a single Verey light exposed them to view; it was the first of countless hugger-mugger burials he would experience at the Front, conducted almost always at night under rifle- or shellfire. Nervy and undignified, every one of these interments mocked the sonorous music and lofty tone of a poem he had loved at school, 'The Burial of Sir John Moore at Corunna'. Nothing he would experience of war in the next four years bore any relation to what he had heard of it in story, poem or song.

He might so easily have joined Pat Sharkey too. Three days later the Battalion stopped to engage the Germans in desperate combat in and around Le Câteau; he was standing in the market square in nearby Caudry in a group of forty men who had been told to wait there for instructions, when a shell dropped beside them; there were screams from the wounded, a dozen and more were killed, and Tom was one of only four who was not a casualty. (At the end of that day, forty more from his battalion were killed or missing.) 'A close shave near Mons,' is how he described the event in a letter, not mentioning that his face had been spattered with the blood and brains of a companion. But how long would his luck last? Would he be here tomorrow? Tonight? That became his and everyone's master thought with astonishing speed.

'They're coming!' An enemy attack, Ypres, 1914. (Steel helmets were not used by the British until 1916.)

The ten days' retreat towards Paris that followed the Battle of Mons has become legendary. This is in part because the BEF succeeded by its rearguard actions in frustrating the Germans' attempt to turn its retreat into a rout, but mainly because of the sufferings endured by the marchers; all of them were driven to the very limit of endurance, and some beyond it.

Tom's battalion was chosen to act as rearguard for the other three battalions in the 3rd Division. When the approaching Germans got near the retreating force, and this seemed to happen every few hours, the Battalion would deploy, dig in and fight back with artillery, rifles and bayonets until the attackers withdrew. Then they would resume marching. They marched night and day, often getting no more than three hours' sleep in twenty-four; and they slept, as they marched, with fixed bayonets. Some men had to be kicked to wake up. It was a singularly fine August, and the heat during the day was oppressive. The cobbled roads and streets were extremely painful underfoot; they were cluttered too with families, mostly women, children and old men, fleeing in terror before the oncoming invaders, their carts stacked high with pathetic jumbles of beds, bedding and kitchen utensils, some with dogs pulling tiny cartloads of family possessions. By the fourth day the soldiers were so tired that they would fall asleep on their feet if there was a brief stop on the road; and by the fifth day many would suddenly stumble and fall drunkenly. Near the end of the first week some simply collapsed and were unable to rise; the rest staggered round them, too tired to step over, let alone bend to help them; if not finished off by the bayonet of an impatient pursuer, they might with luck be taken prisoner and survive the War. At one point Tom's company was stunned when their eccentric, beanpole commander, Captain Bowen-Colthurst, whether from the effects of this march or shell shock, turned a crazed eye on his men and abruptly ordered them to march back towards the enemy; they obeyed until the Battalion commander was alerted and reversed the order. It was not the kind of thing you could write home about, remarked Tom to his brother Eddie when on leave. (In another regiment retreating by a different route, two men who could endure no more threw themselves into a river, and a sergeant who tried vainly to save them nearly drowned himself; in the same regiment one man ran screaming in the night from his trench and shot himself; another followed suit the next day.)

Hungry and exhausted, the people on the roads who once fêted them now resented their jostling presence. A child clutched Tom by the leg and begged for food; he gave him one of his regulation rock-hard biscuits, but in fact the soldiers themselves were hungry all the time, denied cooked meals, existing on insufficient rations, and driven to hunting for fruit and vegetables in the gardens of abandoned houses. They were thirsty all the time, too. A large number of houses had bottles of wine stacked outside their doors, perhaps in the owners' hope of deterring looters, or of slowing down the pursuit; but the retreating soldiers were forbidden to touch this tempting largesse.

More afflicted than their stomachs however were their feet. Each night Tom took off his boots and socks and rubbed his soles with petroleum jelly, a tin of which he had had the (chiropodist's) foresight to take with him; but on the third night his feet had swollen so much that he had the greatest difficulty in getting his boots on. Others were less fortunate. Some who were unable to put them on again exchanged them with the refugees for slippers or canvas shoes. Others simply threw them away and swathed their bleeding feet in their puttees, those long strips of cloth wound spirally round the leg from ankle to knee; since they had been told at the start of the retreat to abandon their packs, picks and shovels, so desperate an act as this was not entirely shocking. Unshaven, dirty and haggard, this unsteady column of men, its marching order quite gone, bore no resemblance to the proud parading army hailed by the people of Avesnes less than two weeks earlier.

Almost everyone on this march was tormented by waking dreams of sensory bliss as they staggered along. Weeks later, they compared their hallucinations. Tom was seated with his uncle and brothers in a meadow in the late afternoon, resting against a sweet-smelling, new-built haycock, laughing with the others as they consumed what their mother had brought them in a great basket: boiled eggs, fresh white soda farls sliced down the middle and filled with butter and blackcurrant jam, pints of sweet tea. Or he was seated with his pals at the end of the pier in Sandgate, looking out across blue waters towards France, an enormous ice cream and a cold lemonade before him. Mind over matter, mind over matter, he would say repeatedly to himself as he emerged from his reveries: conscious always that sergeants must not lose control or be seen to weaken.

Every day some were killed or wounded or missing, for the German artillery and infantry kept coming back at them; every day the roll-call got shorter. But from time to time an energetic sergeant would manage to start them singing; Tom's platoon was blessed with a rifleman who could give them a lift with favourites such as 'John Brown's Body' and 'The Minstrel Boy' on his mouth organ ('Tipperary' [1913] and 'Pack Up your Troubles' [1915] had yet to appear in the Battalion's repertoire). They consoled themselves too with the knowledge that they were frustrating a much larger and better equipped force, though they were still puzzled and angry that they had been made to retreat. They were only half-satisfied when on 29 August a despatch was read to them from General French explaining that the BEF was on the west of a kind of horseshoe, and that the purpose of the 'retirement' (as he called it) was to draw the Germans right into it so that they could be 'nipped off'.

Their experience in the forest of Antrecourt near Noyon on 29 August seemed to epitomize their feelings of the moment, and indeed their feelings about the War for years to come. The Battalion reached the edge of this forest in the late afternoon and was ordered by the divisional commander to take up a defensive position there. Fearful, however, of being lost in the forest at night and being picked off by German patrols seen in the area, the Battalion commander, Colonel Bird, sent a messenger asking his brigadier for permission to move before sunset. This request was refused and a midnight march through the forest was thus forced upon the Battalion. The colonel was fortunate to find two local foresters to act as guides; and then could be seen an extraordinary spectacle. Two long files of soldiers, each led by a forester and *an officer holding a candle*, each soldier holding on to the one in front of him, trekked slowly through trees and undergrowth. They emerged before dawn, lucky that the mist rising from the valley of the River Oise below, which met them in one great enveloping cloud, had not yet penetrated the forest and defeated even their guides. What better image of the years ahead?

The terrible march drew to an end on 5 September after they crossed the Marne, blew up the bridge behind them, and billeted outside the little town of Chatres, a mile or so south of Paris. Except for those unfortunate enough to be chosen for sentry duty (in another retreating regiment two sentries had been tried and executed for falling asleep on duty), they enjoyed two full nights' sleep and one day's rest. The first of two batches of reinforcements arrived, 210 in all, indicative of how many casualties they had suffered since Mons.

That evening some of the marchers, washed and shaven for the first time in weeks, wandered into Chatres, an unexceptional little town graced with an ancient cathedral of improbable splendour. Tom and a friend went in and sat down for a while at the rear. From the far end drifted the sound of voices: women and children reciting the rosary with a priest, a monotonous but soothing chant familiar to Irish ears; more welcome at that moment, he would say, than the sound of any choir. The setting sun illuminated the magnificent stained glass on the western wall behind them and pierced the gloom of the ancient building with shafts of golden light. The two young men were silent when they came out, troubled in soul by the disconnection between the calmness and splendour of that place and the violent life they now lived. They would see many beautiful old churches in the towns and villages of France and Belgium, before and after destruction, all so unlike the drab modern constructions in which Irish Catholics were accustomed to worship. They would see their glorious intricacies of art in stone, wood, paint and glass reduced to rubble and ashes by the relentless battery of screaming shells.

5

The Germans had overstretched themselves in their drive south and now had huge problems of supply; an Allied counter-offensive began, and the pursuers who knew that Paris had been within their grasp became the pursued. They were defeated by the French at the Battle of the Marne, and for five consecutive days were driven further north by an elated and reinvigorated BEF. According to the British command, the tide had turned. To be used more than once in World War I, the tidal metaphor, which can imply ceaseless repetition and sameness as well as reversal and change, was much more appropriate than was understood at this time.

The Germans were driven back across the Aisne, but they stopped there and dug in with great thoroughness, determined to hold their line. On makeshift bridges and under constant fire, the British regiments managed to cross the river; however, the Germans held commanding positions on the sloping ground on the other side and inflicted serious losses with heavy bombardments and wickedly effective machine-gun fire. Every attack made by the 2nd Battalion was repulsed or answered with an even fiercer counter-attack. One such counter-attack was a response to Tom's strange company commander, Bowen-Colthurst. His instability showed itself yet again when he took his men further forward into enemy lines than he had been instructed, capturing and losing German trenches; the result of his audacity was that four officers and about seventy-five NCOs and men were killed or wounded. (During the 1916 Easter Rising in Dublin, to which city he was posted presumably 'out of harm's way', he personally murdered some innocent civilians and ordered his obedient men to do the same; among his victims was a well-known pacifist, a gifted friend of the young James Joyce.)

The Battalion was now having a foretaste of the worst that lay ahead. The weather had turned cold, it was foggy, it rained heavily all the time, and for five days they were pinned down in muddy trenches and dank caves by a hurricane of well-aimed metal. At night the wounded groaned in No Man's Land, sometimes within a few yards of the trench ramparts, and the brave risked, and in some instances lost, their lives attempting to bring them in. For the 2nd Battalion, the Battle of the Aisne lasted one week, during which time 46 men were killed and 238 were wounded, their admirable commander, Colonel Bird, being one of the latter.

But there would be another Battle of the Aisne (April–May 1917) and yet another (May–June 1918): the ever-turning tide in a sea of blood and mud. This would be the inglorious pattern of the War: attack and counter-attack, a kind of violent stasis ended only when one of the two exhausted armies succumbed before the newly acquired, numerical superiority of the other. And already, less than three weeks after the Battle of Mons, the cost of this great futility was huge: to say nothing of French and Germans casualties, and ignoring 'normal' interments, the bodies of 3888 British soldiers killed in this short period were destroyed beyond recognition, their only remembrance a name on a single monument at La Ferté-sous-Jouarre on the banks of the Marne.

6

Re-crossing the Aisne, they retraced their steps for a week and then headed north-west, marching by night and then travelling by bus and train until they reached Flanders. They were now taking part in what has been called The Race to the Sea, an attempt to outflank the Germans and prevent them from cutting off the British lines of supply on the Channel coast. The British First Corps was to attack the Germans at Ypres, the Third at Armentieres, and the Second (to which the 2nd Battalion was attached), further south at La Bassée. The objective of the Second Corps was to drive the Germans from La Bassée and proceed eastwards to take the industrial town of Lille. All three offensives have been collectively termed the First Battle of Ypres.

The La Bassée offensive began well for the 2nd Battalion on 12 October. They drove the enemy from the village of La Couture, and then pressed on from village to village over the next seven days until it was about to take the commanding ridge of Aubers, from which an effective attack on La Bassée could be mounted. There had been stiff resistance all the way, but it did not tell against the superiority of the Irish regiment in numbers and close fighting. However, on 20 October German reserves arrived in great number and counter-attacked against the Second Corps

all along the line. The 2nd Battalion was ordered to withdraw and consolidate at the village of Neuve Chapelle. No division or regiment in the
Second Corps would ever get to La Bassée, much less Lille. Thus so far
as the Battalion was concerned, the so-called Battle of La Bassée should
have been called the Battle of Neuve Chapelle. Here its advance once
more became retreat, and its mounting self-confidence (for those few
who survived) collapsed. The Battalion had had a grim experience at the
Aisne, but at Neuve Chapelle it was virtually annihilated.

Neuve Chapelle, to which they withdrew on 22 October, was a
charming village with a fine Norman church, a well-made school and,
on an incline at the northern edge, an elegant château. Some damage
had been done to the shops and houses in the main street, but otherwise
the village was in good shape. Save for the curé and a handful of old
people who had taken refuge in the church, it was deserted by its thousand or so inhabitants. The frightened remnants were advised to leave;
at Captain Dixon's request, Corporal John Lucy (in his best Munster
French) explained to the people that there was nothing the priest could
do to save them if a bombardment started, the Germans returned, and
street fighting broke out. Led by the curé, a rheumaticky old man in a
shabby cassock, they gathered their things and departed sorrowfully.

The château became the Battalion headquarters and location for
the first-aid post. Trenches were prepared on the eastern skirts of the
village, at a distance of about 300 yards, with shallow communication
trenches leading to them. Three of the Battalion's four companies ('A',
'B' and 'D') were sent to the trenches; Tom's company, 'C', was kept in
reserve and billeted in the school.

He was one of the first to enter the building. There was writing
still on the blackboard; the inkwells of the little desks were almost full;
copybooks lay open; there was a boy's jacket on the floor. He stood and
looked round for a moment and against the distant rumble of artillery
he could almost hear (he wrote home) the children's voices; he might
have been back in Derrytrasna reciting his tables for Miss McConville
or a poem for Master O'Hare.

*Christ surveys the ruins at Neuve Chapelle, 1915. Courtesy
of the Imperial War Museum Collection, London.*

Most of the NCOs soon realized that tactically Neuve Chapelle was
not a good defensive choice for the Battalion, for it put them in the line
of fire of 8th Brigade battalions positioned rear-left of them. There was
some artillery-fire from the Germans on the first night, but the killing
was done by jumpy Britishers down the line who shot into Irish patrols
sent out to locate enemy machine-gun emplacements and wandered
too near to them. More serious instances of 'friendly fire' would come
later and add to the sense of lethal confusion that would characterize
this battle. On the following night (23 October) the Germans attacked
with rifle and bayonet, but as at the start of Mons, line after line of the
enemy was mowed down by the quick-firing riflemen in the trenches.
The prodigality of the German staff officers with their mens' lives was
appalling; when it was all over the silence until dawn was punctuated by
the cries and moans of the wounded who lay among the heaped dead.

But on the following afternoon the Battalion's position became the chief target of the heavy guns firing from around La Bassée. From huge howitzers, massive high-explosive shells weighing 858 lbs rained down on the terrified riflemen, four at a time, drowning the noise of shrapnel shells, closing up trenches, sending up gigantic clouds of soil, blowing trees and bodies and body parts like the contents of a giant's waste-paper basket in all directions.

This apocalyptic barrage lasted for an hour, and when it ceased, petrified survivors got ready for the inevitable onrush of the enemy's infantrymen. They shot as many as they could, and when the rest came close went over the top to meet them with steel in the gathering dusk. All their intensity of the last hour exploded in rage as they shouted and swore and stabbed and stabbed again. German bodies multiplied on the muddy uneven ground, but it was a see-saw affair, advance and retreat for an hour. Then at 6 pm the remaining Germans withdrew.

The next day (25 October) 'C' Company came up to replace the dead and the wounded. It was another terrible day. The bombardment was even heavier than before, and it was worsened by British shelling that fell short of the German lines into the Battalion's trenches; casualties were heavy, and the Battalion's two machine guns were put out of action. Germans who had hidden in houses near the left flanks of the trenches rushed the end trench and had to be driven out in savage close encounters by some of 'C' Company, with assistance from a platoon from the Lincoln Regiment, for news of the Battalion's desperate plight had reached division headquarters.

Things got even worse on the following day. 'A' and 'C' companies were sent back for a rest to Richebourg St Vast, some two miles behind the line, but were unexpectedly recalled that evening. 'B' and 'D' had been swallowed up in an enemy attack which swept into the village from its north-east end; every member of these two companies would be reported missing. Half the village was regained by 'A' and 'C' in a terrible dogfight from house to house, but there seemed to be no hope of retaining that portion, much less of regaining the rest. What was left of the two surviving companies – two officers and forty-six men out of around 400 – withdrew to Richebourg. With the arrival of other regiments to replace them, the battle would drag on for another two days, but Neuve Chapelle was lost to the Germans. Being the likely locations for artillery emplacements and battalion or company command posts, the church, the school and the château were inevitable targets for the increasingly accurate German artillery and so were left in ruins; the rest of the village was in flames.

The bodies of the dead officers had been laid out neatly on the château lawn for burial but were abandoned thus in the pressure to escape the oncoming Germans. Buried, however, behind the school wall under a thin layer of soil and stone and a makeshift wooden cross was the body of Rifleman John McAlindon, service number 6826, a distant relative of Tom's from Lurgan. He was bayoneted on the 26th in a terrible scramble in the back room of a house on the village's main street but lived long enough to whisper something incomprehensible about his mother in Tom's ear. Four days later, when billeted in a farm outside Locre, west of Ypres, Tom sat down in an empty kitchen and wrote a letter:

> *The British Expeditionary Force*
> *Northern France,*
> *1 November 1914*

Dear Annie,

I am sure you will have received the telegram by now that brought the terrible news of John's death. I cant tell you how sorry I am. When I answered your letter two years ago I did say I would look after the lad and in simple ways I did. But out here things are not what we ever dreamed of in peacetime. There are some simple things you can do here to avoid the worst, but after that its a matter of chance. John was a lively lad but he never did anything foolish or took unnecessary risks. The company was caught up in a terrible attack and John was one of many who were killed in it. He fought and died very bravely. I was with him at the end and you were his last word.

I'm sure you will feel bitter as well as sad and feel that his young life has been wasted. I know that at home many are beginning to say that Irishmen should not be fighting England's war and that their cause is not ours. Some of us do think and worry about that in the Battalion and our only answer is that Germany is an invader and that we Irish have a lot in common with the French and the Belgians and that the conduct of the Germans especially in Belgium has been shocking. To try to drive them out of these countries must be a good thing. We never thought of these questions when we enlisted at seventeen, it was just a job and a bit of adventure. It's a lot more than that now I'm afraid.

I feel in a way that I am talking to my own mother and apologizing to you both. When I see you opening that telegram I imagine her doing the same, something I dread for her sake, and so my pity for you is very great.

What more can I say except that I loved John like a younger brother and would want you always to remember that he was a good lad, brave and reliable and great craic and very popular with the rest of his platoon.

> *Yours very sincerely,*
> *Tom McAlindon*

He sealed the letter and put his head in his hands. After some time he looked up to see the farmer's wife standing quietly nearby. He pointed to the letter and struggled to put together some words from his phrase book: *La lettre est pour la mere d'un soldat mort.* She nodded sadly and held up two fingers: her two sons had been killed in *la guerre*, she said. Mothers and fathers and the maimed, he would say, were the chief victims of this war: the dead were dead but the living wounded would suffer forever.

The village of Neuve Chapelle would be fought over furiously once more, and effectively obliterated, in March 1915. Such was the ferocity of the bombardment then that the decomposed bodies hastily buried there by the Germans after the first battle, and even bodies in the local graveyard, were disinterred in the earth's upheaval, mingling with the new dead — 115 men from the 1st Battalion of the Royal Irish Rifles. Like so many others, young John's body would never be identified nor given a marked grave. He is remembered only as one of the 13,479 men whose names are inscribed on the Le Touret memorial for missing soldiers killed in this area between October 1914 and September 1915.

Although the Battle of La Bassée (or the First Battle of Neuve Chapelle) was a failed attempt to break through the German line, it was construed by General Smith-Dorrien, the corps commander, and reported in *The Times* and *The Irish Times* (24/25 November), as a 'splendid feat' and 'an enemy attack repulsed with great gallantry'. The heroism of the 2nd Battalion in preventing the counter-attacking Germans from extending their line beyond Neuve Chapelle had to be recognized, just as the scarcity of genuinely good news had to be disguised. The general's compliment was read out to the paraded Battalion in June and inspired as much sarcasm as satisfaction. 'Fine words from the big fellas in the big châteaux,' said Sergeant Martin Butler to Tom. The official praise heaped on the fighting men throughout the War, turning costly defeat into moral victory, too often seemed like attempts to distract attention from the fact that they were the helpless victims of military and political blundering. Martin Butler was killed in the trenches a few weeks later.

7

The remains of the Battalion marched north on 1 November 1914 in time to join in the last phase of the battle to defend Ypres, a much more ferocious and extensive affair than La Bassée had been. Passing through Ypres en route to the trenches at the village of Hooge, four miles to the east, the men were impressed by the tidiness and liveliness of the town (people still going about their business despite the distant roar of artillery) and by the medieval splendours of St Martin's Cathedral and the magnificent Cloth Hall. Like the rest of the town, these great buildings would soon be rendered little different to the last place they had 'defended'.

Some time later, Father Gill, the newly arrived Catholic chaplain, a chatty Irishman and a knowledgeable Cambridge graduate, remarked to Tom and a few others that in the lovely old Convent of the English Ladies (Les Dames Anglaises), which they passed on their way, hung the standards of the Irish Brigade that fought with distinction for the French against the English at the Battle of Fontenoy in 1745. But oddly, he remarked with a twinkle, fifty years later the Irish Brigade accepted the invitation of England's German king, George III, to join the British army. An uncle of Daniel O'Connell, Ireland's Great Liberator, was, he thought, its general at the time. 'And here we are,' he added, fighting for both the English and the French against the Germans. 'I told him I took his point,' wrote Tom, 'and that I once had a teacher just like him. History is bit of a muddle, full of surprises.'

Ypres had the misfortune of being strategically situated on the roads leading to the Channel ports in Belgian Flanders and so was in the way of the advancing Germans in their 'race to the sea'. On the night of 11 November, the French and British units holding the line to the east of the town, facing a better equipped and numerically superior force, were subjected to the heaviest bombardment the British had ever known; this was the prelude to an attack at Nuns' Wood (Nonne Bosschen) by the Prussian Guard, an elite regiment of the German army. Every available man was thrown into the line by the British – cooks, engineers, medical orderlies, batmen. Those who were not killed by the shells or buried alive when the parapets caved in resisted firmly, speed and accuracy in rifle fire being their major strength. As on previous occasions, the German command assumed that the huge casualties taken by their infantry were due to machine-gun fire (at this stage in the War British battalions still had only two machine guns each as against thirty held by every German battalion). The 2nd Battalion's main contribution to the day's combat was to resist a second attack launched at dusk, losing a quarter of its fighting strength in this encounter. The Germans finally withdrew, but the slaughter on both sides had been huge. Throughout the night the survivors were subjected to the now familiar torture of listening to voices in No Man's Land calling in English and German for help or, more pathetically, for 'mother'. Again, this torture drove some men to fatal extremities of valour; a few others it drove literally mad.

Those who endured and survived the First Battle of Ypres thought of themselves as a special group and would always be held in high regard by their fellow soldiers. How much more so those who held the coveted Mons medal as well: in the 2nd Battalion, however, these were very few, and hardly a 'happy few'. In billets at Westoutre on the 20th, 'The Battalion,' says its War Diary laconically, 'was now 40 strong';

three months ago it had numbered 1100. Every one of Tom's nine wide-eyed pals from 1911 had perished by now. Billy C was gone, too, disintegrated by a high-explosive shell from a German trench mortar, the fearsome *Minenwerfer*. Of officers and NCOs there were now only five or six; and by no means all of the forty survivors were from the Regulars who had set out from Tidworth in August. The old Battalion was dead, would never be the same again, and the reservists who were being drafted in to reconstitute it seemed to the old hands poor stuff, hastily and badly trained, rotten marksmen, undisciplined. It was made clear that the duty of the remaining Regulars was to act as models and lend support in every possible way to these raw arrivals.

Of the experienced officers who were brought in at this time, one whom Tom would speak highly of was Gerald Achilles Burgoyne, his new company commander. An Englishman of distinguished lineage (there was one general and one field marshal among his forebears), Captain Burgoyne's second forename correctly predicted at his christening in 1874 that he would become a dedicated warrior. He had come into the Royal Irish Rifles after sixteen years with the Duke of Cambridge's Own Regiment and the Dragoon Guards. He was impressed by the courage and infuriated by the sloppiness of his Irish Irregulars in 1915 and came down heavily on their indiscipline; his rebukes were fierce, and he stunned his NCOs by sending a dilatory private flying with two to the chin, then kicking him till he scampered away in terror. But the men soon realized that he meant what he said when he told them that his insistence on discipline had their safety in mind: in their first month in the trenches, a sizeable number of them were killed by carelessly exposing themselves to view. He liked but understandably disapproved of the popular Jack Whelan, a captain from Belfast in whom he seems to have seen a touch of the lackadaisical Irish and a poor example to the men. Whelan was drafted into the 2nd Battalion from the 1st on 2 November and five weeks later was killed by a sniper while scouting with dog and rifle behind his trench in broad daylight and in full view of the Germans sixty yards away.

But if he preached and practised self-preservation, Burgoyne also set an example of selfless courage. On the night of 18 December, at Kemmel in the Ypres Salient, he went to great lengths and risked his own life in No Man's Land to bring in two wounded Scotsmen who had lain in the cold and wet for five days and nights, abandoned by their own regiment: they were in great pain and tormented by thirst. Burgoyne's style, brisk and curt, concealed a compassionate nature. It was reported by one of his fellow officers that the military honour that gave him most satisfaction was an ivory-inlaid chair presented to him by a Boer widow in South Africa; it was a token of gratitude for not carrying out an order to burn her farmstead, an action that would have left herself and her children homeless. He rose even higher in Tom's estimation when this was told; Tom's own mother, her husband now dying of cancer, and with three children still to be cared for, was never far from his mind.

After the Battle of Nuns' Wood, the Battalion settled down at the beginning of December 1914 to six months of what the regimental historian Cyril Falls called 'routine trench warfare' in and around the Ypres Salient, defending a battle front that extended south for over 590 miles. The change from moving to static warfare had clearly begun, and in the historical imagination is forever associated with that area in particular.

Through constant bombardment, what has been described by one military historian as the dreariest landscape in Europe was by now denuded of every tree and house, every shrub and blade of grass, turned into a brown moonscape of shellholes and craters. It showed the Montiaghs at its flooded worst to advantage, said Tom. Because the water level was so high, the trenches here were of the most elementary kind, two feet deep and in these wet winter months filled with freezing water more often than not; they were essentially ditches behind huge parapets topped with clay-filled sandbags and constructed with firesteps and loopholes at regular intervals. Unable to sit or stand up straight, wet to the knees, and always in danger of being picked off if they forgot to bend, the men would spend two thoroughly miserable days in the 'fire' trench one mile in front of the shattered town of Kemmel, followed by two in the support trench 500 yards back, and then two in reserve at one of the town's last intact buildings, after which they made their perilous return by night to billets in Locre, Westoutre or Dranoutre, some 2–4 miles away. These trenches were gradually improved by placing boards and fascines along the bottom and sides and introducing half-barrels with a board across, an invention that allowed a man to sit with his feet on a dry surface.

The desolation of the landscape around the Kemmel trenches was rendered ghastly by the remains of earlier encounters. Rifles, helmets, belts, knapsacks, boots, tangled masses of wire, shattered planks and upended limbers were scattered everywhere. Bodies lay spreadeagled on the barbed wire before the German trenches; one was perched in the fork of a blasted tree, arms akimbo, legs missing, staring heavenwards, blown there in the blast from a high-explosive shell. Thirty yards in front of the trenches occupied by 'C' Company lay the decomposing bodies of more than a dozen blue-clad Frenchmen, killed at the start of the German offensive in October, their hands and faces now almost black; they had fallen in a neat slanting line, victims of a machine gun enfilading them from one side to the other. Farther out were heaps of Scotsmen mown down in a more recent clash; they were still there as late as April, by which time the omnipresent rats had had their fill of them. And half-submerged in water at the bottom of a shellhole near 'C' Company's front trench was the bloated body of a German soldier. The stench of rotten flesh was all-pervasive.

Bodies and body parts were literally everywhere; this war occasioned a desecration of the human form as no other has done before or since. Trenches would be shelled and mortar-bombed before being assaulted; attackers would hurl in grenades on arrival, and their frantic movement within would be obstructed by the wounded and the dead. Disposing of corpses while waiting for a counter-attack was a problem that called for desperate measures; they were shoved into the rebuilt ramparts, slumped on top as added protection, or buried in the trench itself. Thus it was not uncommon to find that rain and movement exposed a leg or a hand reaching out from the rampart. And there was worse: 'I looked down once more and realized I was standing on a man's face.'

During these four months of 'routine trench warfare', the newly constituted 2nd Battalion was being allowed to settle in and was not involved in offensive action; casualties – usually about three or four killed and seven or eight wounded each week – were caused by sniping, shellfire, stray bullets, exposure, dysentery. The latter was caused by drinking water from a stream fouled by an unseen corpse; even the dead could kill.

On 30 January (1915) a shell fell in the front-line trench, blowing two men straight out of it; they got to their feet, ran around dazed, stopped, and were easily picked off by the Germans opposite. But life was even more uncertain in the reserve trench and the back areas than up front, for apart from the incessant attempt of the artillery to knock out their opposite number behind the lines, or to demolish battalion and company headquarters, there was the constant danger of being hit by stray bullets coming over from the German front line, where the opposing trenches were having a go at each other. In Kemmel on 17 February, Tom was advising Rifleman Ennis on the use of whale oil to prevent trench foot (it was now freely available); he looked round to answer a question from another man, and when he turned back to Ennis there was a whizz in the air and the lad's temple burst open. Death would come with sinister casualness and ironic effect. On 15 April Major Alston, the Battalion commander, was observing the enemy's position through a periscope in a fire trench when a bullet aimed for the top glass of this newly introduced device missed the target but hit a sandbag and was deflected downwards, killing the major instantly. On the makeshift table he had been using in the dugout lay an unfinished letter to his wife; it began by recalling that 'today is the third anniversary of our wedding'. His was the one burial which Tom remembered as having any due solemnity.

Those resting in reserve or permanently engaged in the back areas were frequently sent up front at night on a working party (to dig new trenches or clear out fallen ones; to carry ammunition, wood for duck-boards, or barbed wire) or a ration party. These were dangerous and thoroughly unpopular duties where casualties were common. Thus Tom to his brother Eddie at around this time:

You asked what exactly I meant by a ration party. No, it does not mean a party with army rations, something fairly pleasant! Quite the opposite. Unless a young subaltern is put on the job, the Company Quarter Master Sergeant and I usually take turns to lead a platoon up the line at night with all the rations for 150 men. (Captain Burgoyne did it once last January to set an example for D company.) That's a ration party. We take heavy wooden cases each holding two precious jars of rum, sharp edged tins of rockhard army biscuits, cases of jam, bags of sugar and tea, sandbags packed with charcoal for cooking. And perhaps for good measure several rolls of barbed wire, horrible to hold, or wood for flooring and firesteps. And all this with our basic equipment — rifles, ammo, trenching tools, iron rations, water etc. Recently we set off in freezing rain at eight o'clock. It was pitch black, we followed the road for half a mile and then cut across ploughed land in the communication trench, about two to three feet deep, with at least a foot of mud at the bottom. You had to pull your foot up hard with every step you took and after every 100 yards of this we had to stop for a rest and to make sure that the last man was still with us. Slush-slop-squelch sounds, groans and oaths as men staggered and fell and dropped their loads and struggled to get up. Then the communication trench disappeared, it had been badly shelled in the morning. I lost direction and took half an hour to get back on to the communication trench. Later I fell full face into a large shell hole, almost a crater, with corporal on top of me, stinking muddy water, rum boxes beside us. It took ages for us to be pulled out and get started again, the men very pleased to have had a rest and a laugh at our expense. Soon they were moaning and swearing again as one or other dropped his burden or slipped or banged his face against the rifle butt in front. Shooting started up in the fire trenches beyond, and bullets whizzed overhead or slapped into the mud around us. Sooner or later it had to happen. One man wounded, one killed, two of his pals very upset. We take the dead man's identity disc, and use our entrenching tools to cover him over with soil and stones, sticking his rifle bayonet downwards to mark the place. The wounded man is hit in the shoulder and says he can make his way back by himself, very pleased with himself in fact, thats his ticket home. And so on we go, getting lost, falling, another man wounded, stuff having to be abandoned by the way, more falling into shell holes, until the sky lights up with flares over the front line and we get our direction, and at midnight we arrive. It has taken us five hours to cover hardly a mile. Too dogtired to return, we scrounge places to sleep, myself in a dugout three feet high with two other NCOs, the men sharing firesteps if they are lucky, sleeping with their feet off the bottom and their backs to the trench wall. I am filthy from top to bottom, and too cold and wet to sleep. We brew a cup of tea at dawn, take our tot of rum, and make our way back, this time a bit quicker as you might expect, hoping to catch a few hours sleep before the next job.

O, I forgot. What do you think of this typical job – deepening an old trench. Does it remind you of anything? One man uses a pick on the heavy clay for two minutes by the watch. A second then gets to work with the spade and throws the earth up eight feet to where a third man spreads it. On and on till each of them could fall asleep standing up in his two minutes of rest.

As you cycle grandly around County Cavan in your nice clean warm uniform looking for troublesome gypsies and drunks or lie in your comfortable bunk in the Bailieborough barracks think of me sleeping in reserve on a straw covered floor, each foot in an empty sandbag for warmth, waking up hardcaked with mud somewhere in Flanders. Next time I write I must tell you about our close friends the rats and the lice. Don't forget to write yourself! Letters keep us going, almost important as grub and rum.

Your affectionate brother,
Tom.

8

Towards the end of April 1915, Tom encountered Captain Burgoyne outside the company quartermaster's store in Dickebusch, west of Ypres. The captain accepted his salute and stopped for a few words. After only a week in command of Tom's company ('C'), he had been moved as OC to unruly 'D' Company, and the experience clearly increased his regard for pre-war, professional NCOs such as Tom. In his uncompromising style he talked about the deficiencies of the new lot, whom he thought he had knocked into shape in the three months since he had taken over. He then went on to opine that the Battalion was sure to be thrown very soon into action on the Ypres Salient, where the Germans had launched another fierce attack, using poison gas for the first time. He felt that, like himself, most of the men in the Battalion were fed up with their present inactivity and keen to 'get at the Bosch'. He sounded gung-ho. Tom wondered if the enthusiasts (Burgoyne included) would have felt the same had they been at Neuve Chapelle, but politely agreed. This encounter stuck in his memory, and partly because of it he would always associate the Second Battle of Ypres with Achilles Burgoyne. Thanks to the discovery and publication of *The Burgoyne Diaries* (London: Harmsworth 1985), we now know rather more than Tom did about the captain's unhappy participation in that struggle, his first taste of serious action since coming to France.

Intense fighting was taking place two miles south-east of Ypres at the notorious Hill 60; this was a modest hump of ground, but of great strategic value in that flat terrain. The Germans had just taken it from the British, and it was now pockmarked with shellholes in which they had positioned well-camouflaged machine-gunners. Below the hill they held trench 46: it had a thick parapet eight feet high behind which their infantry and more machine-gunners waited for the inevitable British counter-attack.

At 2 pm on 6 May, the four company commanders of the 2nd Battalion received a message from the corps commander, General Smith-Dorrien, telling them they were to take over some trenches near Hill 60; they were to assist a regiment from a different division (the 5th, their own being the 3rd) and should first proceed to its brigade headquarters for instructions and guides. There followed for the four officers a hot and muddy tramp along dangerously exposed roads in the Salient, past all the debris of the recent fighting; they were particularly shocked to see a dressing station where men walked about with seeming indifference amongst lines of corpses, with no signs of impending burial. At division headquarters they were told they were to relieve the Bedfords, who had been in the trenches at Hill 60 for twenty-five days, and given a guide to take them there. Being within rifle fire of Hill 60, the four men and their guide proceeded cautiously, with intervals of fifty yards between them, and eventually arrived to discover a ghastly scene. There was a mass of bodies, some mutilated and many showing the distressing effects of poison gas. Grass and foliage were everywhere bleached white or sickly yellow. In crowded trenches the Bedford men crouched low, clearly demoralized and impatient for relief. These were trenches 47, 48, 49 and 50, regularly enfiladed from Hill 60 and trench 46.

Inspection done, the four captains then made their way to the Bedfords' battalion headquarters where they were instructed to go back to brigade headquarters to meet up with their own battalion and receive their orders. They arrived at 8 pm, wet and muddy after a fall into a ditch, and lucky to have escaped the usual evening 'hate' fire from the enemy; they were also very hungry, not having eaten since breakfast. They were kept waiting in a scullery for two hours, after which they were brought by their Battalion commander, Major Weir, to meet the divisional commander. The general told Burgoyne that as a preliminary to the taking of Hill 60, his company would occupy trench 47 and then seize 46 at 2.30 am sharp. A simple job, he said, just fourteen or fifteen men with bombs and bayonets would do it; Burgoyne was given two boxes of the primitive and complicated 'jam tin' bombs, a type he had never used or even seen before. The general's battle plan, he noticed, was drawn up on the back of an envelope.

The Battalion arrived to join their company commanders at 10.30 pm. They had left Dickebusch at 3 pm and marched to a certain cross-roads where they were told to await the arrival of guides. But cross-roads were favourite targets for the enemy's artillery, and they were lucky that a shell which landed in their midst was a dud; moreover, the guides did not arrive until 9 pm and during the long interval they had been standing around making tea and (wrote Father Gill) singing dismal songs about ill-fated warriors; black humour being, of course, a form of protest. The guides took them by a route along which lay wounded and unwounded men, the unwounded coughing up white froth from lungs lacerated by chlorine gas. Footsore and hungry (they too had not eaten since breakfast), they reached the trenches at 1 am. The Bedfords, however, were slow to vacate the trenches, being fearful of enemy fire. Moreover, they had not buried their dead, and part of the rampart in Burgoyne's allotted trench was blown in. For tired and hungry men, it was a thoroughly bad prelude to an attack on Hill 60, scheduled to begin at 2.30 am.

Burgoyne was very angry when he saw the condition of trench 47 and tore into the young subaltern in charge about the unburied dead and the broken parapet; he felt that 'no battalion should have got into such a demoralized condition'. But he was joined by Valentine Gilliland, a

25-year-old captain whom he described as 'absolutely invaluable'. Young Gilliland had twenty-four hours to live (a sniper's bullet was waiting for him in trench 46) and he clearly had that possibility in mind. Around midnight at headquarters, he had managed to dash off a letter to his widowed mother in Derry, telling her that he was going into action. She would receive it on the same day as the telegram informing her of his death.

With Gilliland beside him, Burgoyne told Captain Leask to collect six of the bravest men he could find as his bombers. They then opened the boxes of 'jam tin' grenades and examined them with the aid of a pocket torch. Neither Burgoyne nor Leask could see how to operate them, so other grenades left by the Bedfords were hastily chosen instead. Leask and his six brave men then went up and over and zigzagged to the great parapet of trench 46; however the firing pins in the grenades jammed, the group retreated, and all but Leask were mown down; he staggered back to Burgoyne, with wounds to head and ribs. Burgoyne's plan had been that he and the rest of the company would follow Leask and take the trench immediately after it had been bombed, but now he saw that attack was futile. The enemy had started up with a cacophony of rifle- and machine-gun fire and was pitching mortar bombs into his trenches. He managed to pick off an audacious machine-gunner but took a slight head wound; a private standing beside him had a hand blown off and was staring at his wrist in disbelief. With its exhausting and confused build-up, a hopeless mess blithely conceived on a scrap of paper, the whole situation suddenly overwhelmed Burgoyne. He couldn't think, he couldn't act.

Although wounded himself, Captain Leask, on perceiving that his OC's problem was more psychological than physical, insisted that he and the injured private should make their way back to the first-aid post. And there, Burgoyne admits in his diary, he broke down after reporting to the compassionate Major Weir. With some officers who were suffering from gas, and many severely wounded men, he was sent by ambulance to the dressing station at Ballieul; it skirted the south and east of ruined Ypres, framed now with scarlet and orange flames in the night sky. From Ballieul he was sent via Le Havre to Osborne, a former royal residence on the Isle of Wight where 'more or less mental cases', he recorded, were treated. In wonder, or pity, or self-absolvement, he noted in his diary that Captains Whitmore and Hutcheson and Lieutenant Norman were also sent home 'broken down': they had endured the bombardment to which the hapless battalion was subjected from trench 46 and Hill 60 for a further four days. Burgoyne would spend the rest of the War in the 4th Battalion in Ireland, training recruits to be drafted abroad.

For Tom and a few other NCOs, Burgoyne's fate was a pertinent reminder of the fragility of even the strongest. The tough captain himself was brought to confront his own limitations, so that there is an entirely uncharacteristic note of humility in the last pages of his vividly written diaries (10 May 1915). However, he and others were understandably bitter about the haste and confusion with which high command had sent them into battle. More of the same, however, was to follow soon for the 2nd Battalion.

9

On 9 June the Battalion was moved to new trenches at the village of Hooge; from here they were to join in an attack on the German line at nearby Bellewaarde Lake, approximately two miles south-east of Ypres and less than that distance directly below Westhoek, where they would be engaged in the Third Battle of Ypres in 1917. But before they set out, copies of the general's message complimenting them once more on their gallantry at Neuve Chapelle ('when they repulsed the enemy with bayonet') were distributed among the companies and read out on parade. This attempt to bolster their confidence and assuage their bitterness met with the now customary sardonic comment from the Regulars: 'More of the old guff.'

Their task was to take Bellewaarde Spur on 16 June, a ridge within the larger range of ridges that overlooked the Allied forces in the Salient. The German trenches were subjected to a preliminary bombardment from 2.50 am until 4.15 am, and then the attack began. The main attack was carried out by the 9th Infantry Brigade, supported by the 2nd Battalion's 'C' Company followed by 'D' on the left, and 'A' followed by 'B' on the right. It began well: the bombardment killed most of those in the first two trenches and demoralized the rest; these trenches were easily taken. But 'C' and 'D' were carried away by their enthusiasm (or success) and, instead of consolidating the first-line trench as instructed, charged on towards the third, getting in the way of the 9th Brigade, whose job was to rush that line. Ordered to return immediately, they sent back a messenger explaining that to do so during daylight would result in many casualties; high command, however, insisted upon their immediate return, and the consequence was exactly as they had anticipated; Tom was one of the few who got back unscathed. Meanwhile, a thick mist had descended, and the British artillery, failing to anticipate the speed of the advance, was shelling its own men. Company 'A' had made it to the first line and managed to consolidate it, but 'B', shelled from both sides, lost heavily and had to be recalled. The survivors lay low in their trenches for the rest of the day, pounded incessantly by shellfire.

Then in the afternoon, the general officer commanding the 7th Brigade received orders (presumably from the distant corps commander) to renew the attack at 3.30 pm. Dismayed, the GOC pointed out that because of the mist the artillery could not give the men the necessary support and that the company commanders would find it impossible to keep track of their units; nevertheless, the order was insisted upon. So the remains of 'C' and 'D' companies, led by Captain Farran and Lieutenant Eales, after thirty hours without sleep and having endured twelve hours of deafening bombardment, repeated their dawn attack, this time without artillery support. As the GOC anticipated, it was a hopeless endeavour. The advance platoons were mown down by frontal and flanking fire and the exhausted and angry survivors fell back into the first German trench, the taking of which was the day's one achievement. From all the regiments involved that day, there were 3800 men killed, wounded or missing, 313 of these being from the 2nd Battalion – almost 50 per cent of the (reconstituted) Battalion. The gain had been 250 yards on a front of 800 yards. And Bellewaarde Spur had not been taken.

Captain Edmond Farran, aged thirty-four, of Templeogue, County Dublin, the leader of the doomed afternoon attack, had been a lawyer in civilian life and the author of several legal textbooks: a distinguished career lay ahead of him had he survived the War (or not enlisted). Informed by the War Office that he was wounded and missing, his sister Elizabeth wrote to the United States embassy and to the War Office in London in an attempt to find out if he had been taken prisoner, but the German Red Cross reported that he was not on their list of prisoners. Moreover, a nurse in Rouen wrote to say that some wounded soldiers in hospital there had reported that he was killed in the attack of 16 June. Elizabeth, however, would not give up hope, but contacted Holywood Barracks in Ireland, where many of the returned members of the RIR could be found. Thus in September she was called to the camp and introduced to Lance Corporal Connor of 'C' Company, who had been in the attack with her brother. Limping slightly and looking ill at ease, he came into the colonel's office and was introduced to her. Very quietly, he explained that he himself had been in a rear platoon and was wounded in the ankle. He lay low for some time and then crawled back to the first German trench. On his way he came upon her brother and two NCOs lying together, obviously the victims of machine-gun enfilading as they led from the front. The corporal was already dead, and within ten minutes the sergeant and her brother died too.

'Reported missing' was a message that gave desperate and often vain hope to relatives (the case of Rudyard Kipling's son, John, is well-known). It was some consolation to Elizabeth that her parents had not lived to endure the loss of their brilliant son, whose future had once seemed so bright. But she would never have the consolation of visiting his grave. Instead, on a visit to Ypres years later she was able (she thought), with the aid of someone's binoculars, to pick out his name among the 54,896 inscribed on the Menin Gate Memorial to those with no known grave. She had been appalled by the waste of one man's life, but there, like every other visitor, she was overwhelmed by the sight of that colossal monument to lives unfinished and undone. It brought home to her 'the absolute insanity of it all!'

For two days and nights, the 2nd Battalion's dressing station at Bellewaarde had overflowed with a constant stream of wounded men. Father

Gill gave assistance to the overworked medical officer and his staff, and only with the greatest effort of will (he wrote) could he endure the sight of so many terrible wounds of every kind: one man with both legs and an arm blown off, some with half their faces gone, one with his intestines hanging out, every imaginable violation of the body. For how long could any individual continue to witness these horrors and hold on to his sanity? And what future, what recognition would there be for those who would go home blind, maimed, disfigured, repugnant to sight? There would be no monument to the multitude who lived out the rest of their lives in the limbo of broken minds and bodies.

True to form, however, their commanders gave a comforting version of the failed attack on Bellewaarde's spur to the survivors and the press. The current Battalion commander, Major Morris, said that 'all companies distinguished themselves by their discipline, coolness and steadiness under the most trying circumstances', and before leaving to assume command in another regiment, he told the men that both at Belle-waarde and Neuve Chapelle they had 'covered themselves with glory' (War Diary of the 2nd Battalion of the Royal Irish Rifles, 23.6.1915). The brigadier general said that the Rifles had made a name for them-selves that 'would go down in history' (James W. Taylor, *The 2nd Royal Irish Rifles* [Dublin: Four Courts Press 2005], p. 67). Later, too, the corps commander sent a message telling them he was pleased to hear of the success of their aggressive operations (War Diary, 6.7.1915). Infected by these assertions, a number of the recent drafts who had come through unscathed wrote boastful letters home about their deeds, excerpts from which were published in the newspapers, hungry for good news. As a matter of course, these newspapers made their way back to the Battalion and were duly distributed by the chaplain. In the sergeants' mess, the heroic letters were ridiculed by the older hands. And in due time not even the rawest recruit would be seduced by the lies of glory. Courage and endurance there was in plenty, but glory none.

10

No 14 General Hospital,
Wimereux,
Northern France.
22 November 1915

Dear Eddie,

You will probably have heard by now from Mother that I was wounded on October 4 but not seriously – nothing to head, heart, or abdomen, just gunshot wounds to the leg and knee. In fact now that I'm out of bed and hobbling around with a stick life is very pleasant. And after what I leave behind, and with all these young nurses to look after me, even life in bed, a real BED, is very agreeable. I have lots of time on my hands now for chatting and reading and I think I might even spread this letter out over a day or two. A friend is going back to base in Belfast next week and will post it for me when he gets there so I can write knowing that it will not be censored, not that I have anything outrageous to say. I am getting lots of practice writing, for quite a few chaps here have hand wounds and need a secretary!

The good news is promotion, from Company Sergeant Cook, not that I did much cooking, to Company Quarter Master and acting Company

Sergeant Major. Which means I'm now a Warrant Officer. There has been a pay increase and so some more to send home to Mother. It's good that between us we are making her life a bit easier. I hear from her that the girls are doing well at school and a great help at home and that the Master says Denie is the sharpest wee scholar he ever had. If I get out of this thing alive I'd like to think you and I could get him a secondary education. A young officer here from Armagh town told me there is a secondary school there and another at Violet Hill in Newry where they take in boarders. When I talk to these chaps from home who got a commission at 19 or 20 because they have a secondary education I begin to realize what I missed out on and have been thinking more and more about education and all the things I don't know. One of the good things about this war and about being a pre-war regular is that the officers are not nearly so standoffish with you as before and we talk more together. We all know how much we depend on each other. All but two of the officers are Protestants, Irish or English, the rest of the battalion is mostly Catholic, but we never talk about Irish politics so that doesn't come between us.

I think my promotion had a lot to do with Captain Goodman, a Dublin man who saw a lot of service in South Africa and India and Burma before he joined us at Dover in 1909. I remember him well from the talks he gave us at Fort Burgoyne about his experiences there, for he got us all worked up about going overseas. He was wounded at the start of the La Bassee battle last October and came back in June. He told me I was the only pre-war man in the Battalion he remembered, all the others killed or gone wounded in the nine months since he left. He said that he and Major Weir our new Battn commander heard how much front line work I had done and so on and would like me to do a lot more. Most of my routine duties as Quarter Master Sergeant could be carried out by my assistants, as the cooking was. So I have been acting CSM as well and been steadily in the firing line.

We had a horrible experience at a place called Bellewaarde near Ypres in June. It was a shocking failure, with heavy casualties, and no fault of the men, if you see what I mean. I still can hardly believe I got out of it alive. We felt very angry about it, well those who lived to be angry, and we simply couldn't believe it when three months later we were sent back to the very same spot where so many of our lads were killed and buried and wounded and told to attempt much the same thing all over again. In the circumstances you would think they would choose another battalion. We had been having a rest behind the line playing football and of all things watching another division putting on a Horse Show, pretending they were in Ballsbridge or wherever, minus the lovely ladies. Then we were called back into the Salient. Fierce bombardment of the enemy lines had been going on, we had heard it day after day, and we knew that something big was up. There was to be a big push against the enemy line from Flanders down to Artois and Champagne. Our job was to join with two English regiments and advance 800 yards from Hooge to Bellewaarde Lake and to keep the enemy from sending down reinforcements to Loos, a more important show.

Although it was still only September, it had been raining and by this time the bombardments had destroyed everything green in the Salient and turned it into a brown shitty mess, with watery shell holes everywhere and spiky black stumps for trees. We attacked the enemy trenches from Hooge, a village now totally flattened from the last time we saw it, you couldn't even make out where the church had been, everything just rubble. We bombarded them for half an hour and let off four mines under them before attacking at 4.20 am. No trouble with the first trenches, most of the men there dead, but by the time we approached the second one all our men carrying the bombs had been carefully picked off by the German snipers and most of the rest were just target practice for the machine guns, especially if they were caught in the barbed wire that the mines and artillery had failed to cut. Without the bombs there was no hope of taking the rear trenches but on we went. Imagine trying to charge carrying over 60 lb of equipment through mud, when you don't lift but PULL every step, when it takes you five minutes or more to stagger out of a shell hole with all that on your back and the groaning bodies of your pals all around you. How long would it take you to cover 800 yards?

The attack was called off in the afternoon. We failed in our immediate objective and although we did prevent the enemy from reinforcing the line at Loos the price to our battalion was about 350 killed, wounded or missing. No Mans Land was packed with the dead and the wounded, but constant rifle and machine gun fire made it impossible to bring in anyone until nightfall. We did the best we could after dark and were relieved at midnight. We got back to camp at 6 am, exhausted and fed up. But alive, the survivors. Next day the Corps commander came to tell us we had fought like tigers and congratulated us on our gallant conduct. Well.

Though I try not to, I keep wondering just how long I'll last here. With my pals from Tidworth nearly all gone, its got to be soon. On the other hand maybe I have a charmed life, as one or two have said to me. Maybe I'll see it out. I wasnt wounded at Bellewaarde by the way. It happened nine days later, 5 October, when we were in the trenches at — you wont believe this — Armagh Wood. To make communication easier the staff officers and their map makers often give Irish and British names to landmarks and roads out here. Funny if I was buried or drowned in a Flanders Mointies. A mortar bomb fell ten or twenty yards away and wounded five of us when I was sharing out the rum ration. The jars were all smashed and the men cursed and swore as they patched us up and sent for the stretcher bearers. The rum tot is precious at night in the firing line when we are cold and wet and sick to the teeth of the filth and the noise, tormented by lice and likely to be sniffed at as we sleep by our close friends the rats already fat on the flesh of corpses.

24 November.

Now about Wimereux. Its a small seaside town, almost a village, about ten miles from Boulogne. The part of the hospital I'm in consists of tents pitched on a big field above the town. From the edge of it you can see the sea and a great long golden beach. After the trenches at Ypres its paradise. Its not officially what we call a Clearing Hospital but its almost that, for most of the cases are arm and leg wounds and are evacuated fairly quickly. Every night two or three convoys of ambulances come and go by road and we can see the ambulance trains arriving by night down on the railway nearby, their front lamps shining like great yellow eyes in the dark. At night too there are the search lights moving around on the lookout for enemy planes or a Zeppelin. Some times they keep moving all night slowly sweeping the heavens. We have them at the Front too but here they seem quite beautiful, peaceful and steady, without the eerie blue and yellow flares that suddenly light up everything in No Mans Land and then fizzle out.

It seems I could easily have been shipped off to England for further orthopedic attention and recovery, but one of the MOs told me that the Battn CO asked them to keep me and two others here if at all possible – shortage of experienced men, I suppose. That suits me, and with luck I might be here for Christmas, for although I am healing quite well I still limp and need a stick and physiotherapy. Most nights we sit around the tables and discuss what we hear from the newcomers and the off-duty nurses join in. Things are not going well despite what the papers are saying at home and we all now think this war will go on for a long time. We are not fooling ourselves any longer nor prepared to be fooled.

But there is a lot of joking and fun, everyone is so glad to be out of it if only for a while. The nurses are a lively lot. They hold parties at night in their quarters and if you're lucky you get an invitation. I met a very nice Welsh girl who seemed rather a laughing happy type but her friend told me that her brother was killed at Ypres, that she is terribly upset and is trying extra hard not to let it get her down. She has black hair and big brown eyes and a wide white smile. Very nice looking. She and her friend introduced me to the Sussex Hotel in town where we had tea a few times – funny the way they give English names to the hotels here. Weak and watery tea not like Ma's but a fine lounge with a view *of the sea. Yesterday she managed a lift in an ambulance for both of us into Boulogne. We had a fresh fish meal down at the harbour and a whole bottle of white wine, quite cheap. Boulogne is a busy bustling place, lots of soldiers of many nationalities. She admired the colourful uniforms and headgear of the French and Indian soldiers but all the while I was admiring her. I'll say no more. She and I know without saying it that I am likely to join her brother in a matter of months. We only ever have today.*

There are things good and bad that I can say to you but not to Mother. I suppose we were a bit like twins in the family. Do keep writing to me even if you dont get a quick or a long reply. As I must have said before, the post is a very big thing in our lives out here.

Your affectionate brother,
Tom

I I

He was sent from Wimereux to No. 3 Base at Boulogne on 20 January 1916 and returned to the Battalion at the front line on 27 February. Presumably he was given light duties at base; what happened between 24 November and his departure from Boulogne two months later, what he did or thought or felt, how Christmas was celebrated, is a biographical blank. Family history comes down to us in discontinuous fragments: the odd letter, a photograph or two, remembered confidences and conversations. And a soldier's regimental record, if it survives at all (which it does in this case), is factually spare and clinically professional.

He reached the Battalion billets at La Crèche, some seven or eight miles south of Ypres, early on a Sunday morning. After Mass he was welcomed back by Father Gill, from whom he learned that his friend Sergeant Frank Doherty (one of the most devout in the chaplain's flock), and their popular medical officer, Lieutenant MacKenzie, had been killed on 28 November; and that Sergeant John Lucy, another of his acquaintances from Tidworth days, had broken down and returned to Ireland almost immediately after that ('suffering from neurasthenia', said the medical board). He would miss kindly Frank, whom he had known since enlisting in 1908, and the talkative, intelligent John. He was beginning to feel, he said, like a man they once saw stranded on the south coast, the tide coming in all around him, the cliff at his back. The Battalion had been emptied and reinforced so often that his own survival seemed almost a mistake, a clerical error in military accounting.

According to Father Gill's unpublished War Reminiscences, the MO was called to attend to a wounded Royal Engineers officer who had been hit while working on a new trench. He set out immediately and came upon the wounded man ten minutes later: 'He began dressing his wounds,' wrote Gill, 'and, whilst doing so, a shell fell killing him and Sgt Doherty. *Both were killed on the spot* [my italics].'

Years later, in the process of explaining his own nervous collapse, John Lucy would provide a strikingly different version of the two deaths. In *There's a Devil in the Drum*, Doherty (whom he calls Ryan – all those mentioned in the book are given other names, though most are identifiable) was not killed at the same time as Lieutenant MacKenzie. Rather, Doherty brought the dead officer's body back on a stretcher to the field-dressing station and asked Lucy to come and look at him – a strange request, surely. Doherty cleaned the dead man's face tenderly, combed his hair, arranged his tie, and asked Lucy to kneel with him and pray, which Lucy did – ' "Pax vobiscum" or "Lord have Mercy on you" ' (he couldn't remember which). They left, and Lucy comforted the distraught sergeant, who then went back to the dead man 'like a dog who will not leave a grave'. But another shell came in, Doherty went out to tend to the wounded, and was killed himself while doing so. Lucy returned later to visit the dead sergeant and his medical officer in the dressing station; he looked wonderingly at them, the English public-school Protestant and the Dublin working-class Catholic lying side by side, and saw in both of them something Christlike. Then he heard himself sobbing, 'My manhood seeped from me.' Questioned later by a sympathetic adjutant who observed his distress, he said he felt the loss of Doherty very much. The adjutant urged him to 'go sick ... go home for a spot of leave and ... forget the war for a bit'. 'I accepted gladly,' he adds. He returned to Ireland and would not see the Western Front again until August 1917, when he would spend another four months there before leaving it for good.

Factual or imaginary, and very different from the chaplain's, Lucy's account of the two deaths serves to emphasize an idea that recurs throughout the memoir and that Lucy sees as epitomized in the 2nd Battalion: a genuine union of English and Irish, Protestant and Catholic. This problematic union became infinitely more difficult for nationalist Home-Rulers such as Lucy and Tom after the rebellion and executions in Dublin in April 1916. Lucy, although always emphatic about his southern Irishness, negotiated the difficulty very well. Having recovered from his breakdown, he assisted at the defence of Trinity College against the rebels but did not refer in his memoir to this awkward phase of his career. He remained in the British army until 1935, and his memoir, published in 1938, is evidence of his unswerving loyalty to the idea of an Anglo-Irish, Catholic–Protestant partnership.

Another purpose served by his graphic and emotive account of the two deaths is to explain the nature of his own breakdown, which he imputes more to grief than to battle stress. This would perhaps make sense in so far as he had not in fact been in the firing line since December 1915, when he was given a secretarial job in battalion headquarters, a post he still held at the time of Doherty's death, even though his narrative appears as always to put him in the military thick of things. It is just as likely however that the constant shelling, which affected those out of as well as in line, was the main cause of his breakdown.

'There comes a point in the career of every fighting man when he can endure no further,' wrote a young infantry officer. 'He may be perfectly healthy, but he knows that the day is surely coming when he will break ... the certainty that the break is coming fills him with dread. Officers who have trusted him begin to watch him – they begin to doubt his courage.' (Quoted in John Laffin, *On the Western Front* [Stroud: Sutton 1985], pp. 210–11.) Such an idea would have seemed particularly relevant two months after the departure of Lucy when the 2nd Battalion was subjected to conditions more nerve-shattering than at any time before. They were moved to the trenches at the base of Vimy Ridge, one of those long, gentle slopes that gave the Germans so much defensive advantage over the British and French forces who tried to push them back. Here there had developed a tense subterranean competition, with each side not only shelling but also tunnelling under each other and blowing up key positions. Without any warning whine or whoof from the artillery, trenches would be obliterated and men buried alive or atomized in a second.

There was constant attacking and counter-attacking to seize and dig in to the great craters left by the underground explosions, and in these attacks the work of the bomb carriers was as crucial as it was perilous. One of the Battalion's bomb carriers was 26-year-old Rifleman Sammy McBride, a Regular who had enlisted in 1911. At Vimy his platoon suffered severely, especially from *Minewerfers*, hugely destructive mortars whose shells could gouge out trenches to a depth of twenty-five feet. Although his platoon commander, Sergeant D. Miller, would testify that he was 'a good and willing worker, both in and out of the trenches', 'an all-round good soldier ... willing at all times to volunteer for any dangerous work to be carried out' (*2nd Royal Irish Rifles*, p. 179), the strain became too much for him. He disappeared on 14 or 15 May, just before the remains of his platoon were called on to go up and over yet another time. Four months later he was picked up, a picture of wide-eyed passivity, in an empty tent at the Canadian Stationary Hospital near Boulogne, and, at 7.10 am on 7 December, he was executed for desertion. Like perhaps many of the young working-class men from the ranks who were executed for alleged cowardice and desertion, had he been an officer, or a bright and articulate young sergeant on easy terms with his superiors, his distress might well have been observed before it became unbearable, and treatment at home for 'neurasthenia' or 'shell shock' would have been recommended. Even that tough and experienced professional, Henry Goodman, who became lieutenant colonel and commander of the Battalion in 1917, eventually found the strain of the front line too much and suffered a breakdown; the Battalion War

Diary simply notes: 'To England 14/12/17. Struck off strength.' The colonel was not told to 'pull himself together' and 'soldier on' but was sent home on sick leave; he did not return and took honourable retirement from the army in 1929.

[25 May] There was absolutely nothing you could do [at Vimy Ridge] but wait and hope your number wouldn't come up. Our artillery couldn't easily locate their emplacements on the other side of the ridge and weren't much use to us when we launched an attack. The ground around us seemed to shake most of the time with explosions above and below. You crouched and waited in your stinking trench — they were stacked with bodies when we took over — till a barrage ended but you could never expect a lull of a few hours as you could when it was routine artillery bombardment. You would wait knowing that any second a mine might explode under you and send you in bits to Kingdom Come. Some of our trenches and the men in them went up in that way. Men would huddle down in their funk holes in the sides of the trenches and some whimpered like babies and got terrible fits of the tremors. One of my old companions [McBride] from far back just vanished and hasn't been heard of since. We heard that another man down the line climbed out and ran screaming up the ridge and a sniper picked him off. I'm sure thats what he wanted, a quick clean ending. Lieut. James Cordner from Derryinver who joined our Battalion only in February broke down and was sent home as a shell shock case. Ma must know the family well. He was a Protestant minister before he volunteered. But his cousin Jack Cordner a machine gunner is still going strong, a tough one and very lucky too. I think he'll outlast us all. Sometimes it was actually a relief from the awful waiting to get the order to attack the enemy who dug themselves in to one of the huge craters the mines made.

Anyhow here I am still, holding on tight, fingers crossed, and there's not much use asking you or Mother and the girls to pray for me. As we often say out here, the Lord must be very busy by now what with the French and the Germans and us all recruiting Him to the cause. I heard a hard case say the other day that He's about as useful as General Haig. Not one for the chaplain! Truth is, all we can do is trust to Luck and keep our heads down ...

12

They withdrew from Vimy on 20 May and for the next six weeks were rested and trained in preparation for a major offensive against the enemy line; it was to be conducted in the valley of the Somme along an eight-mile stretch of the Front ten miles south-west of Vimy. The long stalemate was to be broken in one ferocious push by the British, with assistance from the French. Continuously for one week, the enemy lines were subjected to the heaviest battery ever mounted by the British, and then on 1 July the infantry were sent forward. Since it was assumed that no one in the trenches could have survived the battery, the men were instructed to go forward at a steady walking pace in straight lines. But the barbed wire had not been destroyed by the field artillery as expected and the trenches and bunkers had been so deep in the chalky soil and so well-made that the assumptions were quite wrong and the instruction (now one of the most notorious commands in military history) fatal. Moreover, the ground on the ridges had been turned to a sea of glutinous mud by the shelling and by two days of heavy rain, so that the work of the German machine-gunners on the high ground, confronted with this slow march of death, was horrifyingly easy. On that one day there were 57,000 British casualties. The

2nd Battalion was not involved, but the 1st Battalion was, losing almost half its numbers (415 killed, wounded or missing). The attack began at 7.30 am and ended at 10 am. The great breakthrough had failed, and the rest of the Somme offensive would be of the now usual attritional kind, with small gains at best and steady losses.

Brought up to full strength yet again by hundreds of new recruits (the old image of cannon fodder is irresistible), the 2nd Battalion was sent in at the end of that dreadful first week. Its task was to join with the two other battalions from its division, the Lancashires and the Cheshires, and on 7 July to take the village of Ovillers, an objective that its sister battalion had had in its sights; from there it was to ascend the ridge below Pozieres and ultimately push east to Baupaume and Cambrai. Ovillers had been flattened by the combined force of the earlier and the morning's bombardment, but its cellars had not been destroyed, and they provided excellent shelters for the machine-gunners 'who were the great stumbling block to success from end to end of the line'. (Cyril Falls, *The Royal Irish Rifles in the Great War* [Aldershot: Gale and Polden 1925], p. 67.) The struggle for this ruined village lasted over a week, and much of the fighting took place during the night and in the most difficult circumstances. Landmarks in what had become a terrain of ultimate desolation had been obliterated; the trenches had been blown in; their chalk bottoms turned to a sticky whitewash that soon smeared the men from head to foot.

They had to contend not only with the machine guns but also with successive counter-attacks in which enemy bombers fought to take back every dozen yards lost. Sometimes fighting for thirty-six hours at a stretch, they would snatch an hour's sleep here or there, their misery compounded by the casualties caused by their own artillery. Stretcher-bearers could not approach from the rear, and the wounded had to lie in the trenches covered by their own oilcloths; most of the dead were heaved up on to the parapet, providing protection for the living. But in the end, heroic resistance collapsed on the enemy side. White flags went up, exhausted Germans emerged shouting, '*Kamerad*,' shaking hands with their captors, whitewashed-grey and whitewashed-khaki, a confused brotherhood of wretchedness and misfortune. For some of the victors, the handshakes set a question mark beside the minor triumph they had achieved. And their renovated battalion was now down to about half its strength. The mincing machine would need more bodies soon.

> [17 July] We had a young volunteer here called Bobbie Kernaghan. He said he was seventeen but looked about fifteen to me. He was just out and so keen to get at the Germans, they had killed his favourite uncle. He was from Balfour Street in Belfast and said it's a small world, a neighbour of his was an Annie O'Hagan from the Mointies. Do you know her? I straightened his pack and checked his rifle (everything we have and wear is plastered with mud) before we went up and over on the 9th. We had hardly gone ten yards when he got it in the chest. He looked like a schoolboy asleep when they brought him in and laid him down. He lay covered over in the bottom of the trench for a few days. Every time I passed him I thought of when I was seventeen and of the nine years I've had since then. You get very callous here after a while, you simply have to, but this lads death got through all my callousness. The Divisional Commander inspected us this morning and congratulated us on our 'great work at Ovillers'. Great!

The Somme offensive dragged on until mid-November in ever worsening conditions. Unusually heavy rainfalls followed by snow combined with incessant shelling, rats and voracious lice to make life in the waterlogged trenches unbearable. Pozieres, the highest point on the contested front, was taken at huge cost by the Australians; but Baupaume, which was to have been captured in the first week, remained in German hands, and Cambrai was as remote as ever. The Allies had suffered 600,000 casualties, around 400,000 of them British, and advanced about seven and a half miles. Some military knowledge had been gained, and some pressure had been taken off the French whom the German high command were attempting to 'bleed to death' at Verdun.

After its opening engagement, the 2nd Battalion was occupied with routine trench warfare up and down the line between Ovillers and Thiepval, mainly in support roles: taking over trenches when won; repairing and deepening collapsed trenches and communication trenches; carrying bombs, small-arms ammunition and petrol cans filled with water up to the front line – dangerous work under continuous sniping and shellfire, every day a death and a wounding. On 24 October they left the Somme and trudged back to Flanders, many of them with a feeling that this war was destined to go on forever.

13

Tom's brother Eddie had joined the Royal Irish Constabulary at the minimum age of eighteen in 1912. He enjoyed his placement as a country copper in Bailieborough, a friendly backwater in County Cavan in which it would seem he was very popular: some of its elderly inhabitants remembered and fêted him when he and Denis paid the town a visit over forty years later. Lodging as he did in the barracks, he was now able to send money home to his mother on a regular basis. In the middle of November 1916, he received a postcard from Tom saying he had ten days' furlough and asking if he could meet him on the 22nd in Belfast. It was not difficult to get two days off to see a brother who had been at the Front for over two years. They spent the evening in The Globe, a pub close to the railway station. It was the busiest and most attractive pub in the city and they knew it well — Eddie had worked there as an apprentice barman before joining the police.

They had much to talk about, common concerns and anxieties. The present was not the future they had envisaged when they enlisted. It was not just that the War had changed the world for everyone; there was the political crisis at home. The Easter Rebellion and the executions of its leaders, added to the determination of Protestant Unionists not to become a discontented minority in a 'Rome-ruled' Ireland, comparable to the situation of the Catholic minority in the subsequently partitioned North, had effectively put an end to the possibility of Home Rule for all Ireland, that compromise between separation and union which the majority of Irish nationalists had hitherto favoured. (IRA-Sinn Féin would come to accept it for Northern Ireland in 2006.) The predominantly Catholic RIC saw themselves as custodians of a future Home-Rule Ireland and for at least fifty years had been accepted by the whole community; now however they were being used by the military to do all the searching of suspected Republican houses and were beginning to be identified with British oppression.

It was a difficult time for the likes of Eddie, and he would in fact leave the police for good in 1921, not long after his barracks had been besieged by a band of Republicans (the young IRA man who shot him in the leg visited him in hospital and apologized, saying it was the inspector he was aiming at!). Exchanging gunfire with his fellow countrymen was not something Eddie had ever contemplated. For his part, Tom talked about the recruitment crisis that the Irish regiments were facing at home, which could only get worse, and about the crisis of loyalties that some of the serving men at the Front were experiencing – what kept them going, he said, was loyalty to one another in do-or-die situations where Catholic–Protestant, nationalist–Unionist differences were of no significance.

Those concerns slipped from his mind when he got off the six-seater sidecar from Lurgan at Derrytrasna crossroads. He went straight into the post office and grocery to say hello to Louise and Sadie Stevenson, the two sisters who now ran it for their father ('A 'clare to God if it isn't our Tam McAlindon!' shouted Sadie, all of a flutter). Then he walked down the slope into Derryloiste. As always on return, as far back as his Tidworth days, he was instantly seized by the remoteness and the quietness of the place and by the pleasant whiff of turf smoke coming from the scattered cottages. He could have known with his eyes shut that he was home.

But when his mother embraced him, he suddenly thought of all the doomed sons in No Man's Land crying 'Mother,' '*Mutter.*' What worlds of difference, what journeys unintended on the high road of youth! His two young sisters clung to him too, and Denis, now a sturdy nine-year-old, stood shyly watching. All Denis's brothers had now left home, and as his mother said, coaxingly, 'Denie' was now the man of the house. No mention was made yet of their father, who died in 1915.

He enjoyed being spoiled by his mother and sisters, and the simple things: sleeping long in a warm, dry bed; fresh soda bread and butter and jam and hot tea for breakfast; craic at night with relatives and neighbours who had heard of his return; falling asleep to the friendly whistle of the crickets in the wall behind the open hearth, audible in his adjacent bedroom. Each afternoon he walked up to the school to meet Denis and talk to the master. The boy went with him everywhere. They set lines for eels in the big drains in the Moss; they borrowed a flat-bottomed boat from the McGeowns and went spoon-baiting for pike on the Bann, Denis seated quietly at the back, holding the line while Tom rowed. He mended fences and did the daily chore of fetching drinking water from the well at the crossroads. He took the wheelbarrow up and down from the Moss half a dozen times every morning until the lean-to at the end of the house was filled to the top with turf.

The ten days flew by, and he was gone. The house was empty, unbearably quiet, everyone lost for words. Would they ever see him again?

14

He rejoined the Battalion in the trenches at Ploegsteert on 3 December (1916). A village at the bottom of the Salient, it stood directly below the shattered town that would be forever remembered as a symbol of the Allies' stubborn and costly determination to block the German drive to outflank the French and cut the British off from their naval lifelines. On their right at Ploegsteert, stretching all the way up to the village of Passchendaele (a little over six miles away, north-east of Ypres), was the arc of commanding ridges overlooking the Salient, held now by the enemy for three years. The ridges were fortified in front by pillboxes, by machine-gun posts embedded and camouflaged in the sides of craters, by barbed-wire entanglements and three lines of trenches, and behind by concrete-and-timber dugouts and heavy artillery emplacements: German efficiency at its very best. Here and there in the swampy land below lay the unretrieved and blackened bodies of French and British soldiers who would be ploughed back into the earth during the bombardments of the Third and the Fourth Battle of Ypres.

When we sat in the babble and smoke of the Globe, and above all when I stepped down the hill into Derryloiste and smelt the turf, I felt I was back in the real world, escaped from nightmare. But now I wonder. This seems real, home a dream. I certainly belong and am needed here. Every month hundreds are drafted into the battalion — more and more from England — to replace the dead and the wounded. Its never the same battalion, but always the same name. Still, the new ones and the rest of us are only strangers for a day or so, and can soon become as close as any friends at home. Major Goodman, Old Tough Boots the men call him, came back while I was away and is now Lt. Col. and in command of the Btn. He gave me a warm word of welcome, talked about main-taining the traditions of the Btn and said the new lads needed people like me badly. That sort of thing keeps you going. The new fellows think the Regulars who've been through Mons and Neuve Chapelle are quite special and really look up to us. Well, we are few enough.

They were needed now more than ever. The worst winter in living memory had begun. Thick snow soon hid the pockmarks and blanketed the dead on the Salient. Below gaunt and shattered poplars, frozen thrushes lay by the roadside between Ploegsteert and Neuve Eglise. The mud at the bottom of the trenches froze hard, but although that was a relief, conditions for the occupants were still ter-rible. Their daily bread, always more palatable than army biscuits, was frozen solid if and when it reached the line. During the long nights, there were whimpers of misery from young men who lay in cramped dugouts and funk holes, shivering, sleepless and afraid. There were three identified cases of self-inflicted wounds: one on 26 January and two the next day, and perhaps several unidentified cases among those who stumbled or were stretchered back to the aid post. Duck boards disappeared and fires were surreptitiously lit, a practice on which the sergeants were told to come down hard ('Mostly, I turned a blind eye'). Hot tea with rum was a great comfort and briefly distracted minds from thoughts of the next mortar bomb, or a sudden bombing raid, or the hidden sniper waiting for an incautious victim. Relatively speaking, it was a quiet time, with no sign of an impending offensive.

But death was always near and carelessness fatal. On the night of Tom's return, Lance Corporal Tom Caldwell was on sentry duty in a shallow outpost when he stood up to stretch himself and was picked off with a single bullet that went straight through one temple and out the other.

Behind the lines on an exceptionally cold morning (15 December), they had been paraded for a solemn announcement, more chilling than the whine of a sniper's bullet. No. 5009 Rifleman Samuel McBride, they were informed, had been found guilty of deliberate desertion, and the brigadier general had judged there 'was no reason why the extreme penalty should not be carried out'. The sentence had been confirmed by the army's commander-in-chief, General Sir Douglas Haig, and he was shot on the 7th. None of the men judged him, however: 'The poor bugger', 'It could be me', 'If I ever look like running, for Christ's sake sock me one and tie me down.'

It had been the duty of a young Englishman, Second Lieutenant Richard Marriott-Wilson, just posted to the Battalion, to serve as witness and see that the sentence was promulgated. He had been transferred early in 1915 from the Royal West Surrey Regiment to the 13th Battalion against his wishes, was wounded and hospitalized in July 1916, and on returning to the Front in August asked to be sent to his old regiment. The request was turned down and he was posted instead to the 2nd Battalion, arriving one week before the execution at which he had to officiate. 'A stinking job, a bad omen,' he was heard to say. He went down with trench fever a month later and was invalided home; but he was sent back in December 1917, to be killed in action with the 2nd Battalion at St Quentin in March 1918, having fought there with conspicuous gallantry, for which he was awarded the Military Cross. He was twenty-two. Like so many others, he had become a fatalist, conscious of subjection to arbitrary power and blind chance. He was also an apprentice poet: among his effects was found the draft of a piece entitled 'Kismet' (Arabic for 'Fate'):

Opal fires in the Western Sky,
For that which is written must ever be,
And a bullet comes droning, whining by
To the heart of a sentry close to me.

For some go early and some go late,
A dying scream on the evening air,
And who is there but believes in Fate
As a soul goes out in the sunset flare?

For the first four months of 1917, the 2nd Battalion spent half its time holding and supporting the front line (while collecting casualties) and the rest of the time in training behind the line. They were to take part in a grand Anglo-French offensive involving thrusts at Messines, Ypres, Arras and the Aisne. This was a prelude to the Third Battle of Ypres, or Passchendaele, which did not commence until June, after the April–May offensives at Arras and the Aisne had ended in costly failures.

For months the men were left to speculate on the likely purpose of all the training. Presumably the Battalion commander had that purpose in mind in February when he filled in army form B.2064, recommending promotion to the rank of second lieutenant for Company Quartermaster Sergeant McAlindon:

> This Warrant Officer was serving in my company at commencement of the war. He served in the firing line as Company Sergeant Major when the Btn. was commanded by Brigadier General Weir, who has a high opinion of him. He is thoroughly reliable and steady and I am confident would make a good platoon commander. I would like to retain him as such in this Battle.

Somewhat to his surprise, Tom felt no sense of strain in the officers' mess, where he sensed that the others – and especially the young subalterns with little front-line experience – regarded the promotion as well-deserved.

Of course I knew very well that the daily wastage of young officers is what promoted me and that it would have taken years in peacetime for someone like me to get this far — if indeed it would ever have happened.

But he was pleased and proud nonetheless, and with Second Lieutenant Paddy McMahon, another Armagh man, and Second Lieutenant Bill Rainey, a recently commissioned NCO from Belfast, he went off to St Omer — regimental headquarters' base — to celebrate. An obligatory part of the celebration was having his portrait taken in his new uniform at Antoine Raillon's studio on rue Carnot. In this portrait his expression is quietly cheerful, with the hint of a smile. For the time being his mood seems hopeful, even confident — unlike that reflected in the sombre 1918 portrait that has haunted me since childhood.

Tom McAlindon, 1917.

Once in the officers' mess he acquired a better sense of what was going on, although the surprise factor in the offensive was a well-kept secret until zero hour. An attack on the Messines Ridge, a strategic position of crucial importance, had been planned for months. Nine divisions were involved under the command of General Sir Herbert Plumer. Seizing this ridge was regarded as a necessary preliminary for taking Passchendaele Ridge and effecting a total breakthrough of the enemy line around Flanders. Plumer prepared for this attack with immense care. A perfect replica of the ridge, covering over one acre of ground, was constructed so that everyone would have an intimate knowledge of the terrain. The key to success was to be a line of twenty huge mines – 600 tons of explosive – placed under the German lines in tunnels extending over 3000 yards, supported by artillery of unparalleled density, with one gun of greater or less size every few yards along the ten-mile line. Of great importance too was the new system of creeping barrage: following an exactly calculated timetable, the range of the artillery would be gradually extended so as to be always in front of the advancing infantry. Colonel Goodman's operation orders, issued to his company commanders on 3 June, clearly reflected the general's meticulous approach to this battle. The objectives for each company, platoon and section; the timing of each unit's advance and the distance between each; what each unit must do when it achieved its objective; the normal rate of advance for the artillery's creeping barrage (100 yards in five minutes); what each company's carrier gang would consist of and what it would carry; and what each rifleman would carry – his pack (containing iron rations, soap and towel, one pair of laces, shaving kit, socks, canteen, waterproof sheet), 170 rounds of ammunition, two (empty) sandbags, two bombs, a box respirator, field dressing, a full water bottle, a pick or a shovel: all this and much else, including the setting of compasses and synchronization of watches, was specified.

And because the general had expressed doubts about the loyalty of some of the Battalion's Irish Catholics, even 'the cause' was specified: 'All ranks are reminded that they are fighting for: (i) The Allied cause of humanity against highly organized, disciplined, and educated savages. (ii) For their women and children. (iii) For the honour of Ireland.' The elegant oxymoron in (i) was an allusion not only to the Germans' much publicized misconduct in Belgium but also to their recent scorched-earth activities when retreating behind the Hindenberg Line from the pleasant area they had comfortably occupied for two years: not only did they raze each village and farmhouse before leaving, they also killed the farm animals, poisoned the wells, and cut down every fruit tree in sight.

From 21 May until 6 June, the enemy lines were subjected to a massive bombardment from 2300 guns and 300 heavy mortars. Then on 6 June, the men were informed that the attack would be on the morrow, and at 5.50 pm they moved from their bivouacs up to the assembly trenches. Zero hour was to be at 3.10 am.

[Fruges, 28 June]

We had known for so long that something really big was going to happen that the waiting that night was the worst I could remember. I doubt if anyone got a wink of sleep we were so tense. Our guns kept up a regular barrage all along the line for ten miles, then they suddenly stopped dead on 2.50 am. The silence was unbelievable. At about 3 am I heard a cock crow in some distant farmyard. Then a few enemy flares sailed up over No Mans Land, everything out there as quiet as the corpses, but the Germans must have guessed an attack was imminent. They would have been stood to and at the ready waiting for us. Then there was the order to fix bayonets and get out of the trenches and lie flat and wait for an explosion — staff were afraid the trenches would cave in on us. It happened at 3.10. I felt the earth move and rock under me, like the floor of the ship on a bad crossing on the Irish Sea. That went on for almost a minute it seemed. I remember that I saw the explosion — all the explosions in one — well before I heard it. I looked up and saw great pillars of orange fire leaping into the heavens carrying huge black masses of earth, cauliflower shaped. Then came the sound, more thunderous I'm sure than has ever been heard on this earth. We read in

The Express *a few days later that the sound was heard in the Prime Minister's study in London. I'm not surprised.*

Each company and platoon moved off in strict order and our guns started up again and the sky behind us was alive with flashing red and yellow all over again. We met no resistance. 'B' company's first objective was a farm heavily fortified with machine gun pillboxes that could have enfiladed the whole line from the right flank; when they reached the position it was not there, it was just one huge crater, the concrete and timber and men gone up in dust. All the front line trenches and the men in them were gone. There must have been thousands who were blown to bits and mixed up with the stuff that clattered down on our helmets. In one of the first intact dugouts reached — a very deep one, solid concrete all round — there were three dead officers seated round a table who hadnt a mark on them, simply killed by the force of the blast. As we neared the top of the ridge groups of terrified Germans came through the dust and smoke with their hands up, about 200 of them. We just waved them on and continued. It was clear they wanted out of it all and would cause no trouble to the men at the back.

The rest had retreated, and it was all over in a matter of a few hours. From the top of the Ridge we had an amazing sight. You suddenly realized it was a beautiful morning, the kind of early summer morning when you go outside and suddenly feel glad to be alive. Behind us was one vast brown mess of craters and shell holes with sprawling bundles of rusty wire, a few upended tanks and patches of broken and blackened trees, and in front was rolling country with green meadows and woods and neat orchards and untouched villages. If I survive this war I'll always remember its shocking contrasts.

Most of our casualties in that show came in the next four or five days when the Germans started shelling our trenches very heavily. I lost two good friends that way on the 10th. One was Jim Kelly, a CQMS who used to exchange duties front and back with me. He was one of the two witnesses who spoke up bravely at the trial of a poor rifleman recently shot for desertion. Jim led a ration party up to the front line on Sunday

morning after Mass and was returning that night when a shell took
out six or seven of them. The other was 2nd Lt Paddy McMahon from
Armagh town, the educated one who told me about the boarding schools
in Armagh and Newry. He had a nice job in the bank in Newry, a job
for life, when he took it into his head in September 1914 to join up and
apply for a commission. He was 28, had no girlfriend, a broken romance
behind him, wanted a change for a while, and was told by the Bank they
would keep his job open for him when he got back. Poor Paddy. He should
never have enlisted. Just think. He could have been a bank manager a
few years from now married to a girl who loved him in some nice wee
town where my brother was the local police sergeant. Ah well ...

About 10,000 German soldiers were killed or buried alive at Messines Ridge, and 7500 taken prisoner. Notoriously, however, General Gough failed to capitalize on the ghastly success of this action, and so the Third Battle of Ypres was delayed for another six weeks. In the interval, there was some more dangerous work for the Battalion up and down the line, followed by two weeks' training in Fruges, a pretty little town, well-behind the line and near to the historic town of Creçy. Scholarly Father Gill paid Creçy a visit, and while chatting after Mass with a few of his parishioners (as he called them) he had some characteristic remarks to make on its significance. It was famous, he said, for a great English victory over the French in the fourteenth century, but in fact the English king was of French descent and had a better lineal claim to the French throne than his French rival. Of course, added the priest, it was those same French-Englishmen, better known as Normans, who changed the course of Irish history, doing to the Irish what they, the Celts, had done to the original inhabitants of the Emerald Isle. It was typical Gill stuff, Tom said, but it was new to the rest of the group, all recent arrivals.

Fruges was a time too when letters were received and answered. Many of the men read each other's letters and got to know their pals' families and girlfriends, a practice that deepened the bonds forged between them by war. Father Gill was in the habit of delivering the mail and did so with a sympathetic and observant eye, always coming up with a kind word – some excuse or explanation – for those whose faces showed disappointment when nothing turned up. One letter that Tom received came addressed in perfect block letters, almost like professional print. It indicated, remarked the priest good-humouredly, the writer's determination to see that the letter would not go astray. Inside, however, the writing was carefully cursive:

[12 June]

Master O'Hare has been teaching us how to write letters in our English lesson and said we could practise sending one to a family friend abroad. Two of us have brothers in the army in Flanders and Jim O'Hara's brother is in the Navy somewhere. A couple of others have relations in America. He said people who have to go away from home love to get letters. But he did not have to tell me that. I remember what you said to us all here. And John Pat says the same.

We are all well thank God. Ma says she is tough as old boots. I never remember her ill. She reminds me to thank you for the money, you are very good, you never forget. So is Eddie. John Pat has now got a job as a clerk in the Canadian National Railway and says that if he doesn't like it there he might go over to America where he has friends in Minnesota.

You were asking Ma about my schooling. Well, I am doing alright and really enjoy it. I like sums and composition. Some of the boys in my class find the sums very hard and the Master gets me to explain to them how I work them out while he is helping the rest. We have started geography and I find that very interesting, especially the way people live in places like China and Africa. I suppose you would have to join the navy or army to get there. I would love to be an explorer like Livingstone, though he was a Protestant clergyman, so that's out.

I can do the milking now. I do it before I go to school in the morning. Ma says the cow likes me much better than Mary Ellen and Annie and that's why we now get a full can, but I think she says that just to please me. The Master sends you his best wishes and says he saw your promotion in the 'Lurgan Mail'. He says he was very pleased for you. We pray for you every night and are impatient for your next leave. That's all I can think of for now. If you find any punctuation or spelling mistakes in this letter you are a clever man for I wrote it in pencil first and the Master corrected them. Ha ha!

Your affectionate brother,
Denis.

At this time also Tom had two letters returned to him from Wimereux, with a covering note from a matron. She was very sorry to have to tell him that Nurse Moran had been killed when an ambulance she was travelling in overturned outside Boulogne:

It was a terrible shock to everyone, though we should be used to sudden death by now. Rose was loved by all, both staff and patients, and is grievously missed. Many a manly tear was shed that night in the wards when the news came through. One must be very sorry for her parents, who have now lost their two only children in this awful war.

Tom was billeted with some other officers in the doctor's roomy house in the main square of Fruges. The doctor was serving as a medical officer at the Front, and his wife, who had been a teacher of English, seemed glad of their company and of a chance to practise the language. She had a piano, and on a few evenings there was music and song, everyone making his contribution. On the last evening a fair-haired young subaltern sang a quaint and very English little song that was new to Tom. He sang it feelingly, as if it had some personal meaning for him. It pleased the doctor's wife greatly, and it moved Tom too, for he remembered the first verse and wrote it in the blank page at the back of his phrase book:

> There is a lady sweet and kind,
> Was never face so pleased my mind,
> I did but see her passing by,
> And yet I'll love her till I die.

15

Every day in the fields and ditches outside Fruges they had been practising and teaching boy-men how to seize trenches and to bomb and bayonet their terrified occupants; thus the return to the Ypres Salient on 14 July was not so wrenching as it might otherwise have been. Behind the line was often another world, but they were never allowed to forget what had become the only reality; they could sleep and feed and play games (football was favourite), but only so as to recuperate and be better able to kill.

Like the Montiaghs, Flanders ('Marshland'), was correctly named. The area covered by the Salient was reclaimed land, criss-crossed by canals, small streams and watery ditches; in peacetime it gave rich pasturing and abundant crops, but daily pounding from 5.9-inch howitzers for thirty-three months, combined with recent aerial bombing, had destroyed its drainage system and churned up the soil and subsoil repeatedly; by now it was a mudland dotted with innumerable shell-holes, often lip to lip. In this condition, it was a demonic partner to the machine guns waiting everywhere in their concrete pillboxes for the footsloggers who toiled up its inclines in their repeated attempts to take the ridges. 'It was only murder attempting to advance against these pillboxes over such ground,' wrote Sergeant Robert McKay, an ambulance man serving with the 36th Ulster Division during the Third Battle of Ypres. (Malcolm Brown, *The Imperial War Museum Book of the Western Front*, revd. edn [London: Pan Books 2001], p. 259.) In very short time, Tom would be in the sights of one of those deadly pillboxes.

A shellhole in Flanders. Courtesy of the Imperial War Museum Collection, London.

Zero day for the big push was fixed for 31 July. Every night for a week working parties of between two and four hundred men from the Battalion laboured in the mud, carrying timber and fascines made of branches and twigs, repairing or laying down roads and tracks between the shellholes and craters. The darkness reduced but did not eliminate the dangers of this work. The men worked in silence, muttering blasphemies when they fell and were dragged filthy-wet out of some unseen shellhole. But enemy scouts were often around, so that machine guns and artillery could find them out; every morning three or four men failed to answer the roll-call, just as every day new lads were drafted in singly or in groups: Haig's merry-go-round, they now called it in the Battalion.

For the last ten days of July, the enemy was bombarded continuously by 3000 guns expending four and a half million shells: the usual preliminary for an attack, although an exceptionally heavy one. The Germans were numerically inferior by now to the British in firepower but kept retaliating in kind. They were well-ready for the assault when it came on the 31st along the ten-mile front; without the underground bombing used at Messines, there was no surprise element. Moreover, the rain befriended them: it began on the 31st, and except for one day of thick fog, it fell incessantly until 6 August. It was the heaviest rainfall in thirty years. At times the attackers found themselves waist-high in the mud and always staggering forward at snail's pace. The walking wounded who lost their footing on the tracks had a horrible death, drowned in the muddy waters of craters and shellholes. So difficult was movement that it took up to eight stretcher-bearers to carry one wounded man. Horses pulling food and ammunition supplies up to the firing line toppled off the tracks, wagon wheels broke with their fall, the animals were drowned or shot. There were tanks, but most of them got stalled in the mud and proved useless. Thus in combination with the rain, the great bombardment that was to facilitate the infantry did just the opposite. Some ground was gained, but impetus was lost and the sudden breakthrough intended by General Haig did not materialize. The rest of the Third Battle of Ypres would be a battle of attrition, attack and counter-attack, and it would drag on until 6 November when British and Canadian infantrymen, exhausted and embittered, emerged from the mud to take the mound of rubble that was once the village of Passchendaele. The ridge was now cleared, British casualties amounting to 310,000.

The 2nd Battalion had been held back for an attack on Westhoek Ridge on 8 August at the bottom of the Salient. This was close to territory that was all too familiar to the Battalion (or rather to some of them). At 164 feet above sea level, it gave the Germans a commanding position overlooking British movements near Bellewaarde and along the Menin Road; it underpinned the whole defence of their line at that point. General Plumer was determined to take it and, as events showed, the Germans were no less determined to keep it. The 2nd Battalion was in fact taking off where others had failed. Before dawn on 31 July, the 1st Battalion, together with the 2nd Lincolnshire and the 2nd Rifle Brigade, had captured the ridge and then lost it later in the day to counter-attacking Germans whose hidden machine guns did deadly work after the creeping barrage of the British had moved on. The 1st Battalion lost one-third of its force in this reversal of fortunes, and now the 2nd Battalion, together with the Loyal North Lancashires and the 11th Lancashires, were to try again.

For the 2nd Battalion, the prelude to this job was grim. They had bivouacked on the night of 4 August under the great ramparts of Ypres, where enemy shelling killed two men and wounded four others. Then at 9 pm on the 5th, they set out for the British trenches below Westhoek, marching in single file, company by company, platoon by platoon, section by section, each man with his 44 lb of equipment. It was slow and extremely hard going in the dark and the mud, and very dangerous. Flares eventually exposed their sinuous progress, and when 'A' Company was passing through what remained of Château Wood they took a severe beating from enemy shelling at Bellewaarde. The rest arrived at battalion headquarters at 12.15 am, after a march of about five miles, which had taken as many hours. Next day they were in line and most of the casualties of the march – there were seventy in all – were brought in. Of the ten who were killed, one was seventeen-year-old Jim McClelland, eldest son of a widow in Newtownards, Tom's enlistment town.

I had told him I spent many a pleasant afternoon in Newtownards and asked him if the girls still paraded up and down in their Sunday best on Sunday afternoons and he went red all over and laughed and said they

*did. But he said as they all do that he was tired of the place and wanted
to see the world. And anyhow there were too many mouths to feed at
home. Well, I understand that well enough. I made the mistake of mentioning to the adjutant that I knew Newtownards well and he landed
me with the job of writing to the mother. Its just about the worst job in
the world. Though mind you, delivering the telegram would be worse.*

On this day too, John Lucy from Cork, now a second lieutenant,
rejoined the Battalion; he looked chipper and sounded nervously eager
to prove himself after his nineteen months in Ireland, where he was
employed doing clerical work at the depot in Dublin and had done
his military bit defending Trinity College against the rebels on Easter
Monday, 1916. Of the pre-1914 Regulars who had been commissioned
from the ranks, John and Tom, and Bill Rainey from Belfast, were now
the only survivors; they were three minor miracles, officered Old Con-
temptibles between whom, one might assume, there was a special bond
of fellowship.

The Battalion held the line the next day, 7 August. During the night,
Lieutenant Edward Brown, second in command of 'B' Company (John's
company too) was aroused by a scuffling noise at the end of his trench
bay; it was a bombing party trying to get through the defensive wire
frame used to obstruct such raids. He alerted his sergeant and dashed
forward with his revolver cocked; the invaders vanished, but not before
lobbing over a grenade that facilitated their getaway and killed Brown
instantly. A Lisburn man, he was a former member of the Ulster Volunteer Force, fiercely hostile to the idea of Home Rule: a bit quick-tem-
pered, but a great soldier and as decent a fellow as you could meet, said
Tom. John Lucy took his place as second in command of 'B' Company.

Next morning, the 8th, the active operation order was passed
down the trenches. They were to attack at 4.45 am on the 9th, their
objectives being to capture and hold a line about 800 yards in advance
of the present line and to take and hold the village of Westhoek (the
remainder of the ridge was to be taken in a follow-up action by other

designated battalions). There would be no preliminary bombardment; the enemy was to be taken by surprise. But it began to rain heavily in the afternoon, and the attack was postponed until 4.35 am on the 10th. Two days of concentrated misery and tension followed. They moved forward to the second line of trenches on the evening of the 8th and were spotted: twenty-one casualties, two killed. The stretcher-bearers, pacifists mostly, toiled and risked their lives as always, struggling to and from the advanced dressing station on the Menin Road. In the trenches, water rose a foot above the duckboards, tea was brewed with difficulty, biscuits and bully beef were consumed standing at firesteps; outside, shellholes spilled over. And, says the Battalion War Diary, 'much preparatory work was needed and time was limited'. Assembly trenches were dug by night; during the day, other trenches were shored up and ladders fixed for quick exits. Each rifleman cleaned and oiled his rifle and checked his equipment; NCOs nagged and double-checked; officers kept going over the plan of attack. No doubt all this helped to alleviate the misery of waiting. Then at dusk on the 9th, they were told to get as much sleep as they could, and there followed the familiar struggle between exhaustion, bodily distress and either excitement or fear.

Returning from the Battalion commander's dugout that night, Tom noticed the slight figure of Private Pat Maguire squeezing awkwardly into a hole he had scooped out of the trench wall below the parapet. He thought a friendly word might help:

'Are you alright, lad, for tomorrow?'

'I think so, sir.'

'Where are you from?'

'Clonroche, County Wexford, sir.'

'Never heard of it! Have you ever heard of Derryloiste, County Armagh? No? I thought not. That's where I'm from. Tell me, how old are you?'

'Seventeen, sir.'

'I thought as much. How did your mother feel about you enlisting? You didn't have to, not like these English lads.'

'Oh, I'd enlisted before I told her. Anyhow, there was no work for me round the place. I tried hard enough. Now I keep thinking of her all the time. She was upset when I left. His Irish Rose, my father calls her. That's her name.'

[27 September]

When I heard that name, I could say nothing, and the lad kept looking at me, puzzled. Then I said, Come on, son. I'll find you a better place. And I found him a spot on the floor of a dugout beneath some snoring corporals.

The Battalion formed up in position of assembly at 3.15 am and was kept waiting for eighty minutes: all were silent, each man hearing the rhythmic hammering of his heart within. The rain had long since stopped and it was pleasantly mild now; a dog barked in the distance and further afield another answered defiantly; a cock crowed, and another; then silence: for country boys like Pat and Tom, distracting thoughts of home. Then the whistles blew, and it was up and over, shouting, screaming, cursing: letting loose the extreme tension of eighty long minutes, working up the aggression, thinking to terrify the other lot. And somewhere in the midst of all that pandemonium was the son of Rose Maguire from Clonroche, hoping to be a man.

The creeping barrage started immediately. 'B', 'C' and 'D' companies went out in lines of platoons in depth: 'C' (Tom's company) in the middle, 'B' and 'D' to the left and right. When these three had taken and consolidated their designated line, 'A' would follow and establish a line 150 yards further on. They met no opposition for the first fifty yards, and then somewhere up front the rattle of a machine gun cut through the whine and boom of the shelling. It was enfilading the line from right to left. Five, ten, fifteen men stopped, spun round, staggered, fell forward or backward. The rest bellyflopped and sought the protection of shellholes; waist-high in water and mud, they composed themselves and, to a man, fired at the brushwood hiding the brave gunner. He went silent. But he had hit among others the son of Rose, now just another name for the Menin Gate; and also the officer commanding 'B' Company. A runner came over to 'C' Company with a message from Colonel Goodman's second in command telling Tom to take command of 'B'. He moved to the left, contacted a few NCOs, and gradually the whole line got moving again. But not far ahead was a pillbox they had failed to spot, so well-camouflaged had it been. It rattled into action and 1–2–3–4–5 men went down in tidy sequence. 'Down, down,' Tom screamed, unnecessarily. What followed is described in the War Office citation for his Military Cross:

> During an attack he was compelled, owing to casualties, to take over a strange company at a moment's notice. Shortly after the attack had commenced he encountered an enemy machine gun which was firing on and enfilading our waves. With great courage and initiative he dashed at it with his revolver and put the team to flight. This prompt and gallant action undoubtedly saved a number of casualties at the most critical point in the attack.

Or, as he explained to his brother:

[27 September]

> It's very nice of course to get this medal but there was nothing special about the 'gallant action', in fact it was a bit farsical. There was a ditch away to our right along the side of the Westhoek–Zonnebeke road. Leaving word with another officer and a sergeant to get everybody to stay put I crawled up it and got round the side of the pillbox. Obviously they didn't see me or you wouldn't be reading this. I simply fired a few rounds through their loophole. Someone screamed and there was a scuffle of feet, voices of several men. The back door was flung open and when I crept round I saw four or five making off into the dark. I had got the gunner, but even if I wanted to, which I didnt, it would have been foolish to chase the rest of the team. I just blew the whistle and B moved up.

Ypres in ruins, 1917. Courtesy of the Imperial War Museum Collection, London.

What happened here was echoed elsewhere on the ridge and in the village. From pillboxes and dugouts the enemy enfiladed the attackers and took many casualties, but they fled or surrendered when the remainder of the attackers approached, most of those who fled running into the creeping barrage. The unusual absence of a preliminary bombardment combined with the ferocity of the creeping barrage clearly caused panic. As a result, the objective was reached by 5.20 am and consolidation of the new line began immediately (it would be successfully extended by other battalions on the 16th). Over the next thirty-six hours, the enemy made three counter-attacks under cover of smoke barrages and heavy bombardment, but they were successfully resisted, albeit at great cost, by machine gun, artillery, grenade and bayonet.

Their mission accomplished, the Irishmen were relieved by another battalion and returned to Ypres; they then proceeded for reinforcement and training to Steenvoorde. Reinforcements were certainly needed, for they had taken 350 casualties, over two-thirds of the force they arrived with. In his eloquent and sympathetic *History of the First Seven Battalions: The Royal Irish Rifles (now the Royal Ulster Rifles) in the Great War* (Aldershot: Gale and Polden 1925), Captain Cyril Falls deems West-hoek to have been 'one of the most splendid incidents in the history of the [2nd] Battalion' (p. 105), and he ennobles the price it exacted by representing it as voluntary sacrifice; loss here becomes a measure of achievement: 'How splendid its self-sacrifice was can only be measured if we consider its losses. They were extraordinarily high, and it is quite clear to anyone examining them that no troops but those of the very highest quality could have achieved what the Battalion did in face of such fire as these losses imply.'

John Lucy's account of this episode in *There's a Devil in the Drum* finds it splendid in a different way. It comes in the final chapter of his widely quoted memoir and figures as the high point of his own personal endeavours at the Front. Although absent from the firing line since December 1915, he conducted himself here with conscious determination and dash: 'One thing I did decide, and that was to go all out in any attack' (p. 361). As soon as he took command of his platoon, he handled it with all the authority of a seasoned general and seems even to have remembered Shakespeare's Henry V on the night before Agincourt: 'I was glad to see my sergeant cheerful and carrying himself well ... Some of the men were rather quiet, and I went along talking to them, and telling them I had done this kind of thing before, and that all would be well. The main thing was to get out of the trench quickly' (pp. 370–1). Up and over, he led from the front, was twice knocked over and many times jostled by concussions from the shells exploding all around him. He advanced so quickly that he soon 'struck hard on road metal – part of Westhoek' and so 'became exhilarated' (p. 373). Later he spied from the top of the ridge a company of German reserves marching in a rather leisurely fashion towards a trench at the side of a high wood (Polygon Wood); he reacted speedily and under his urgent direction ('Come on. On to 'em') his riflemen took out fifteen of the enemy; had their Lewis gun not jammed, he adds, 'We might have knocked out a company.'

At this point, he writes, his company commander (Captain Richard Jeffares, here called Collins), although wounded, caught up with him and good-humouredly pointed out that all the other platoons were behind him and that he 'had better get back', he had 'gone too far forward. This surprised me,' writes Lucy, 'and at the time I could only feel foolish at being carried away by the excitement of the attack.' And back he went, with 'but eight left out of thirty', a measure of the intensity of the fire he had faced.

So ends his account of the Westhoek attack: there is no mention of the counter-attacks the Battalion had to deal with during the rest of the day and the day following: 'We were relieved that night and marched back … to rest and reorganise. Collins was taken to hospital.' In a personal memoir it is perhaps understandable that no sense is conveyed to the reader that there are four platoons in a company, and four companies in a battalion, or that the achievement of the first as of the second day was a great collective effort; understandable too that time and event should be so contracted.

Immediately after his account of Westhoek, Lucy abruptly tells of a curious encounter with a temporary captain 'called Jackson'. He describes him as 'a doughty fellow', 'one of the bravest officers I knew', who wore no less than 'three decorations for bravery'. 'The troops adored him … he was always ahead of his men pistolling and bombing the enemy.' Nevertheless, this man 'broke down embarrassingly' in Lucy's company and confided to him that since Collins's departure he had become nervous and fearful of going out on night patrol. He begged Lucy to transfer to his company and join him on these patrols. Lucy politely refused, pointing out that he was now second in command of his company and had many privileges. He adds that in his view Jackson was addicted to patrolling and much too keen 'to keep up a name for being outstandingly aggressive'. Predictably (we are to understand), he was killed four months later in hand-to-hand fighting with enemies who fought as 'excitedly' as himself. Whatever other purpose it serves, this anecdote seems designed to suggest that medals and acclamation are no guarantee of real soldierly worth, or perhaps are not always given to those who truly deserve them. Lucy is asking us to look beyond surface appearances in the evaluation of what men are and do.

That being so, it may not be out of place to raise some questions which those experienced in military historiography might be better able to answer than the present writer. Lucy says that 'directly in front of my platoon was the village of Westhoek, which we would take in our stride', and later he intimates that he was the first to reach it. But the battle orders and the Battalion historians put his company ('B') on the left, 'C' in the middle, and 'D' on the right, directly below Westhoek. If any platoon had the distinction of taking the village in its stride it would surely have been a 'D' platoon. Collins (i.e. Jeffares) presents a problem too. The records show that the officer command-ing 'A' was acting Captain McArevey; that Second Lieutenant Wallis took over command of 'D' before or during the attack when its com-mander, Captain Morgan, was killed; that Second Lieutenant Walsh of 'C' did the same shortly before the attack began when his OC was killed. Then there is 'B', Lucy's company. It seems unlikely that any company commander, let alone a wounded one, would chase after an audacious platoon commander to amiably inform him that he had over-shot the mark and left the other platoons behind; he is more likely to have sent a rifleman. But that may be an irrelevant point, for if there was any company commander for 'B' at this advanced state of the attack it was not the wounded Jeffares but Second Lieutenant McAlindon. A simple process of elimination shows us that 'B' has to be the 'strange company', which, according to the Military Cross citation, Tom took over at short notice. The Battalion Diary would seem to corroborate this: 'An enemy MG which had just come into action on the left ... was successfully dealt with by 'B' Coy. 2nd Lt T. McAlindon leading a deter-mined rush put the team of the gun to flight.'

So abruptly and inconsequentially attached to Lucy's account of his own dashing performance at Westhoek, the anecdote about the funky bemedalled hero who sought his help is problematic too, and for this reason: the records show that no officer in the Battalion with three decorations (or two or one) for bravery was killed four (or five or six) months after Westhoek. So far as can be determined, there is no evidence for the existence of anyone matching such a person in the 2nd Battalion other than in Lucy's narrative (for a list of awards and decorations, and biographies of officers who served in that Battalion, see the invaluable Taylor, *2nd Royal Irish Rifles*, pp. 163–4, 191–334).

Lucy's oblique point about the insignificance of awards for bravery may have something to do with a ceremony that Colonel Goodman in the Battalion War Diary records as having taken place behind the lines at the mining village of Raimbert on 26 September. It was an award ceremony for acts of bravery done at Westhoek. The Military Cross was awarded to: 'Major R. de Rose [Goodman's replacement on the ridge], Captain J.B. McArevey, Captain T. McAlindon, Captain G.E. Lindsay (Royal Army Medical Corps), Second Lieutenant T.C. Wallis, Second Lieutenant R.S. Walsh' – Walsh, Wallis, and Tom being rewarded for conducting themselves so well as stand-in OCs (Tom had been appointed acting captain on 23 August).

Second Lieutenant Lucy was not among those honoured that day, and he never did collect an MC or a DSO. But despite his debunking of the mysterious 'Jackson', he was not indifferent to honours and distinctions; nor did any disappointment at not receiving an award for bravery diminish his affectionate loyalty to the RIR. When at the end of his clerical stint in Dublin he received a commission, he was delighted, noting that although 'this was a great honour at any time' for an NCO, 'in war a commission in one's own regiment is a distinction'. Once commissioned, he says, he was urged by a colonel commanding a battalion in the Munster Fusiliers to join that regiment – in commercial parlance, he was head-hunted. 'The temptation was great,' he explains, for it was 'a splendid regiment' and he himself was a southerner, but 'I did not want to break my association with the Ulster men, who were my friends and whose ways I knew' (*Devil in the Drum*, p. 353). Thus when returning to the Battalion before Westhoek, he was moved by the

warm and respectful gestures of some 'old friends' who recognized him
– a sergeant major, a battalion runner, a clerk and 'a muddy rifleman'
(*Devil in the Drum*, pp. 365, 368).

'Old friends'. Neither here nor at any other place in the book is there
an allusion to anyone who might resemble Tom or Bill Rainey, two officer
companions who had been lowly rank-and-file men when he joined in
1912, and who remained while others fell away: the only men in the
existing group of officers with whom he could truly identify after his long
absence. Did he not have a special bond with these unique survivors?

At any rate there is clear evidence that he made use of his relation-
ship with Tom at this time. Following immediately on his anecdote about
the 'windy' be-medalled officer, he says that he left for home towards the
end of October and that on the night before leaving he lost every franc
he possessed at the medical officer's roulette party, so that 'I had ... to
borrow from the MO.' One would have thought that he was more likely
to borrow from Tom or Bill to fund his leave than from a senior officer
whom he had met for the first time little more than a month before.
Perhaps he did borrow from Bill, but he almost certainly borrowed from
Tom. At the end of Tom's regimental record kept in the National Archives
in Kew, there is a copy of his will, leaving everything to his mother, and
two frayed pages listing all his worldly possessions. On the first of these
pages is recorded with painful precision every single item of uniform,
clothing and toiletry, together with his medals (the 1914 Star and the
MC), his camera, his dictionary and a few other books and some letters
(all of this was sent to Derryloiste in the black wooden trunk that lay
funereally in the house for very many years, his name stencilled neatly
thereon in faded white paint). On the second of these two frayed pages
is a list of his savings, all in war bonds, to which is added at the end: '1
cheque D/X658517 by John F. Lucy, 2nd Lieut, 2nd Royal Irish Rifles,
value of £3' – the equivalent of £120 in today's (2008) terms.

Lucy's celebration in 1938 of the 2nd Battalion in *There's A Devil
in the Drum*, and of himself as one of its plucky and devoted members,
would have been greatly appreciated by the regiment, which was by

then assimilated to the Royal Ulster Regiment and recruiting for another world war. When he rejoined as a reserve officer a year after the book's publication, he was made a staff officer, and a year later was appointed training officer in command of the 70th Young Soldier's Battalion, being accorded the rank of lieutenant colonel. Listening to him by day, and reading his book by night, the young men in that battalion would surely have been much in awe of their eloquent commander, and glad to have chosen the Ulster regiment.

16

It is an understandable paradox of military life that it should show in acute form the natural human longing for permanence and unity in a world of change and conflict. Removed from the anchorage of home and country, witness to the destruction of villages, towns and cities, and living with violent death, the soldier clings to the security and familiarity of his unit – section, platoon, company, regiment, brigade, division – much as a castaway does to his raft on turbulent seas. This attitude operates from the bottom up: from the rifleman who antici-pates returning from leave, to his section pals, to the colonel who cher-ishes the traditions and achievements of his battalion, to the general of his regiment.

So the regimental historian Captain Cyril Falls writes forcefully in 1925 that when in October 1915 the 2nd Battalion was moved by high command from the 7th Brigade of the 3rd Division to the 74th Brigade of the 25th Division, 'It was torn from its roots with a venge-ance.' In World War I, he adds, 'Divisional *esprit de corps* became almost as important as regimental, and it was most unfortunate when it had to be broken on occasions such as these.' As carnage and destruction spread, this response to enforced restructuring became more obvious, notably in a feeling of consequent alienation and even contamination. Predictably, the fact that the two major forms of Christianity have always regarded each other as wicked, or spiritually corrupting, or profoundly misguided, could increase this problem for the 2nd Battalion; and of course the religious divide was actually or potentially reinforced by the political.

Consider the perspectives of Father Henry Gill SJ, and Lieutenant Thomas Witherow, son of a Presbyterian minister and subsequently one himself. After the Battle of Cambrai at the end of 1917, the illness and departure of the Battalion commander, the Protestant Dubliner Colonel Goodman, inspired these melancholy reflections in Father Gill's War Reminiscences:

> He had done excellent work and had the interest of every man at heart. All were genuinely sorry at his departure. His disappearance was typical of the sudden changes which took place during the war ... When the time came he said to the next in command as he entered the dugout, 'Is that you? ... Well, I'm off,' and thus ended his connection with the Battalion during the war. Nothing makes one feel far from being indispensable better than war.

When he became chaplain of the 2nd Battalion in December 1915, Father Gill had noted that 70 per cent of the men were Catholics, mostly from the North, but among the officers – 'very decent fellows' – there were no Catholics, except two promoted from the ranks; clearly he felt that at that time a spirit of mutual respect and tolerance prevailed in this polarized hierarchical order, and it would seem that he regarded Goodman as one of those commanders who fostered it. A natural Home-Ruler himself, Father Gill deplored the Easter Rising and feared for the divisive effect it might have in the Battalion at a time when cohesion was of the utmost importance. At the start of 1918, when the Battalion had been drained and reconstituted many times over, with only Northern Irish Protestants and English recruits coming in, he noticed a great diminution in the number of his co-religionists; though there is a consolatory note in his negative report, since smaller numbers meant an increase in togetherness – 'We [the Catholics] are even better than family, I think.' But he found worse changes ahead. The Battalion was moved from the 74th to the 108th Brigade and from the 25th to the 36th Ulster Division. When the Battalion joined the new division, he complained, no notice was taken of their arrival. 'Having been "old soldiers" and used to a considerable amount of notice and congratulations,' this indifference was resented; even more resented was the fact that the divisional commander made slighting comments when he did address them. Moreover, the (Protestant) men in the new division decorated the billets in this commander's honour with the Red Hand of Ulster rather than the 'the sign of our old division', the harp – which was promptly restored when he left. However a month later the chaplain seemed pleased to record that whereas 'when this Ulster Division came from Ireland their boast was that there was not a single RC in their ranks', now, with the assimilation of 'five ... old regular battalions which had no sympathy whatever with the religious or political aims of the original Ulster division', there were between three and four thousand Catholics.

Lieutenant Witherow understandably reacted differently to these changes. In 1912 he had collected 22,160 signatures, mostly at Westbourne Presbyterian Church, for the Ulster Solemn League and Covenant, which pledged opposition by all means to 'the conspiracy to set up a Home Rule Parliament in Ireland', 'at bottom a war against Protestantism'. He detected a comparable conspiracy at work in the new army structures. The 6th of February (1918), he said, would always be for him one of the most depressing days he had ever come through, for on that day they had

> received orders to join the 2nd Battalion Royal Irish Rifles which had some time previous come into our Division ... We were such a happy crowd that it is difficult to realize the feeling of depression that settled down on everybody at the thought of parting ...We were looked down upon as strangers by most of the officers who were not Ulster Division officers at all and who were not inclined to

look at things from the Ulster point of view. They were most careful to distribute us all over the battalion so that we could not collect together as a clan. (Quoted in *2nd Royal Irish Rifles*, p. 112.)

But a much worse change was in store for the men of the 2nd Battalion, both Catholic and Protestant: a change that would render such differences utterly trivial to the few who were lucky enough to survive it. The long awaited German offensive, a mighty onslaught that came perilously near to turning the tide for the last time, began on 21 March (1918). On the 17th, St Patrick's Day, the Catholic members of the Battalion came together for Mass for the first time on that day since 1854, 'a fitting prelude to the terrible moments that were coming', wrote Cyril Falls (*History of the First Seven Battalions*, p. 139). But for those who prayed for his protection, the intercessory powers of St Patrick initially proved as nothing against those of St Michael, the archangel and patron saint of Germany whose name was the code name chosen by the German commanders for their last offensive.

At St Quentin on 21–4 March, in what has also been called the Second Battle of the Somme, the Battalion was cut off from all support at the village of Cugny. Though they were running short of ammunition, they were told to hold the village at all costs. But they were subjected to a violent barrage of artillery- and machine-gun fire, supported by an attack from low-flying airplanes. Then came the German infantry in overwhelming numbers. Rather than wait for the end, the men rose from their trenches to meet them with bayonets. They fought to the last. Of the whole 750, only a few came back. Comparing it to the many times when the Battalion had been gradually renewed before, a distraught Father Gill described this change as a 'sudden extinction'. The Battalion would be rebuilt again on the basis of its remaining eight officers and forty men (most of them returning from leave, courses and various assignments), with huge drafts of half-trained seventeen- and eighteen-year-olds rushed in from the reserve battalions. Instead of the hundreds who filled the church on St Patrick's Day, there were less than thirty when Father Gill said his next Mass: a group of profoundly depressed and weary young men, each thinking of the friends right and left of him who were no more.

Tom was not among the worshippers on that Sunday. Nor, however, was he one of the St Quentin casualties. Nor was John Lucy. We must retrace our steps from March 1918, when the Germans were close to victory, to the last months of 1917.

17

Although Passchendaele and Westhoek were taken, the Third Battle of Ypres as a whole achieved little, and that at a huge price in terms of both casualties and morale. High command and the government hoped, however, that this grim disappointment for the people at home would be offset by victory in the last major battle of the year, an offensive launched thirty miles down the line at Cambrai, twenty miles north of St Quentin. Supported by infantry and a creeping barrage, tanks attacked here in huge numbers, and for the first time on the kind of firm ground that allowed these lumbering monsters to do themselves justice.

Without any initial barrage to forewarn them of an attack, the defenders of the seemingly impregnable Hindenberg Line were astonished on the morning of 20 November when 324 tanks came grinding and creaking through the mist, tearing down deep masses of the heaviest barbed wire as if it were cotton thread. The result that day was a rout for the British, with five miles gained and 4000 prisoners taken. Church bells rang out in England for the first time since 1914 and the newspapers trumpeted 'The Greatest British Victory of the War'. But the celebrations were premature. There were setbacks on the second and third day, with a crucial failure to seize high ground, and a series of fierce counter-attacks from the Germans. Within a week the enemy had recaptured almost everything they had lost. High hopes foundered.

One of the German counter-attacks was at the village of Moeuvres, an important point on their line of defence slightly to the west of Cambrai. Several Irish units were involved here. On 22 November the village was seized by the 12th Irish Rifles, with considerable difficulty and without either tanks or artillery to support them; but two enemy battalions counter-attacked and caught them in a pincer movement, forcing them to withdraw if they were to avoid capture. The Irish Fusiliers launched another attack in the afternoon but were beaten off, leaving many of their wounded and dead entangled in the wire fences that had so seriously impeded their advance.

It being late November, the weather had turned wet and cold. The 2nd Battalion had spent three miserable nights in the open on standby when on the 23rd they were called on to support the 12th Battalion in a much bigger attack on the village. British artillery bombarded it from 9 am onwards, and the enemy counter-bombarded. Little was left of Moeuvres when at 10.30 am the 12th went forward, preceded by a creeping barrage. But so strongly held was the second German line that they could not get behind it. At 2 pm the 2nd Battalion was sent in. By making skilful use of cover, and by fighting, bombing and bayoneting their way through trenches and from one ruined building to another, they had captured three-quarters of the village by 3.30 pm. But the Germans were waiting for them at the north end with machine guns thickly embedded on either flank, supported by artillery-fire. By this time the attackers had taken heavy losses – among the 2nd Battalion, 121 were killed, wounded, or missing; as on the day before it became a choice between withdrawal or extinction within a powerfully supported pincer movement.

So ended Cambrai for the 2nd Battalion, and so ended 1917: a black year for the Allies, and little better for the Germans. It did not end well either for John Lucy, who was so severely wounded on 7 December that he saw out the remainder of the War at home in Ireland. Nor did it end well for Tom:

[2 January]

I was leading my section round by the church in Moeuvres to get at a sniper and an MG man who were doing real damage when a shell burst behind us. Shrapnel tore into my backside and right thigh. I fell flat on my face and felt as if the pain itself would blind me or kill me. I've seen wounds a thousand times worse but I understood then why so many of the poor buggers look at you so desperately and ask you to finish them off. Two of the lads applied a field dressing to stop the bleeding and then dragged me behind a low wall and left me there. I waited till the action moved further up and then half crawled and half staggered back a few hundred yards and passed out. I woke up on a stretcher, face down, a position I've had to get used to. Two brave and gentle lads got me to the regimental aid post where I was injected with morphia. I was soaked in blood but I could see that there were others as bad and some far worse. I can't remember how long it was until I caught sight of them laying my pal Bill Rainey on a table. He was a dreadful mess, one arm missing, a huge stomach wound, his innards hanging out. He was making terrible animal-like noises and blood was coming from his mouth. The MO tore open his vest and injected morphia and when that seemed to have no effect he poured chloroform onto a cloth and pressed it down on his nose and mouth. Then he went quiet. When the MO got round to me I asked would Bill pull through and he shook his head. They had covered him up and placed him outside with the other bodies by the time they got me out.

I keep remembering one day years before the war when we had a sing-song in the pub in Amesbury and I sang 'The Sash'. Bill was a bit of an Orangeman and he said how the hell did a Catholic know all the words of that great song and I said 'Oh, I fell in with bad company when I was a wee lad.' He laughed and laughed and said 'Put it there lad, I'm your friend for life.' And he was. He saved my life at Neuve

Chapelle. Its hard to think of going back and him not there. He was two years older than me and has a wife and a widowed mother back in Belfast. I think I know them almost as well as family — that's the way it is out there, you have quiet times when you share a smoke and talk a lot about home. If I can, I'll go and see them, I know he would like that.

They took me and half a dozen others in a field ambulance to the hospital in Amiens. They X-rayed me and put me to sleep and removed the shrapnel bullets and a shell splinter. Very kindly they wrapped up the bullets and strapped them to my arm — not the sort of souvenirs I'd want to keep. By the middle of December the wounds had healed reasonably well and I was entrained and shipped to Havre and South-ampton and London. I was examined here [Mason's Hospital, London] by a Medical Board a few days after Christmas and they decided I'm not fit for 'active duty or sedentary employment' but should be sent on to an officers convalescent hospital. I think it will be Harrogate up north. I have to confess my problem is not just physical. I'm nervy and very jumpy and hardly ever sleep more than an hour or so at a stretch. I keep seeing Bill. But don't give Mother the details. I just tell her how lucky I am to have got a Blighty that'll probably send me home for a while.

One of the nurses here is Welsh, I recognized the accent, very like the Cork accent, musical, lilting. I asked her where in Wales she was from and she said 'Oh you wouldn't know it, its a little town called Mold.' I asked her did she by chance know anyone there called Moran. She said she knew a Moran family and was at school with one of them, Rose Moran. That knocked me back. Now I keep asking this nurse to tell me more about her, what she did, anything. When I wake up from nightmares in the dark, where I see Bill and all the others, the wounds and the mutilations, I ease my mind by thinking of her and what might have been. On my way to Harrogate I might go to Mold if I can manage it. I would love to see where she grew up.

He left Mason's Hospital in London on 9 January, having been assigned to Furness Auxiliary Hospital in Harrogate. He took an indirect route, catching an early train to Crewe and another from there to Chester. Everywhere he noticed how kindly and deferential the people were towards him, something which all the military experienced at that time (before the War soldiers were regarded with indifference if not contempt by the general public). He still limped slightly and used a stick, so an elderly gentleman seized his valise and ushered him on to the train; a mother made her son give him his seat; passengers asked him questions about how the War was going. What could he say? They lived in another world, he wouldn't know where to begin, and anyhow they wouldn't want to hear it all. He smiled always and relied on hopeful generalizations. They were pleased just to have talked to him and shown their concern. At Chester he stayed the night in a small hotel run by a Scottish family next to the station and was in Mold by midday on the 11th.

In London, Nurse Ruthven had told him how to find the house. Her parents were in their sixties, grave and polite; the father, now retired, had been the head of a local school. Tom told them he had got to know Rose while he was convalescing from an earlier wound at Wimereux and was shocked to hear of her death. He didn't want to intrude but he thought he would call just to say how sorry he was and to let them know how much loved she was by everybody at the hospital. Rose, he said, had told them about her brother, and he appreciated how much they had been through.

He knew that families sometimes were cold and resentful towards the visiting soldier-friend who had survived when their own boy had not, as if he had been unfairly favoured at their son's or brother's expense. But he detected no such feeling here. They seemed pleased as well as sad to talk about her and asked him to stay for lunch. Later he had the courage to tell them that he loved her and that he intended to ask her to marry him when the War was over. They looked at each other and at him and smiled wistfully. Perhaps they took to this pleasant young officer, not Welsh, but Irish, almost the same. The mother said that that would have made her very happy, and the father nodded agreement. Their reaction gave him a strange happiness. It was as if he had proposed, and she had laughed and said, 'Of course.'

They made him stay the night, and he slept in her brother's room. On the wall was a picture of Paul in his Royal Flying Corps uniform: the same eyes, the same colouring, the same expression; it was uncanny. There was a picture of a university rugby team; silver trophies on a shelf, one for the 100-yards' sprint, others for the long jump. What had the parents to look forward to now but their own end? There were no other children. There would be no grandchildren to inherit their memories and his trophies and medals and their thoughts of what might have been; no one to say, 'What were they like? Tell us about them.' They asked him to write to them and hoped he would come again when the War was over. He said he would, but knew he wouldn't.

'When the War is over.' One heard that phrase again and again now; it carried a desperate longing.

Mold, Manchester, Leeds, Harrogate. He enjoyed the travelling, the friendly deference of strangers, bustle without stress and danger, undemanding change. At Furness Hospital he fell in with a group of convalescent officers, most in their early twenties, who spent their mornings rambling on the Stray, the spa town's great open parkland, and having thin Camp coffee in one of the grand hotels overlooking it. Some of the officers recalled a golden past when their parents and grandparents frequented this fashionable resort and rubbed shoulders with the nobility of Britain and Europe at the races on the Stray and at the theatre and the Turkish baths. As in Hyde Park on that oh-so-distant Sunday morning, he caught the air of a world as far from his own as could be imagined. He referred laconically to his origins, and their condescending banter was tempered by respect for his campaign ribbons (they knew of no one who had been so long at the Front); by their shared suffering – the wounds, the nightmares, the fits of trembling; perhaps too by regard for his quiet self-respect. One man remarked that most of them would not be alive if it were not for the Regulars and the NCOs: it was they who 'ran the show' and helpfully explained to the subalterns what to do. They themselves went to war knowing next to nothing. There were murmurs of assent. It was good to hear said what everyone knew.

On 24 January he went before a medical board at the Furness. It recommended three weeks' leave; after that he was to report to the reserve regiment in Belfast, the 3rd Battalion: 'Wounds are healed but he is debilitated,' it said; he 'should be re-examined in two months.' At home in Derryloiste, he felt listless in a way he had not known during his first leave. He had to push himself to undertake the little jobs that needed doing around the place. Denis and he now shared the same room, and the boy would sometimes come over and shake him in the night when he was groaning and trapped in some nightmare. 'Wake up, Tom! Wake up! It's only a dream,' he would say, and light a candle. He would get Tom to tell him again about the strange antics of the platoon's pet dog, a Belgian stray, 'a mangy wee beggar'. And Tom would get Denis to read for him a poem or a story from his school reader. Thus they both got back to sleep. Wise beyond his age, said their mother, which was true in many respects; he had the maturity born of premature responsibility as well as of an unusual intelligence.

Long since out of practice as a cook, Tom now enjoyed making the family dinner and trying out his mother's recipes for soda farls and apple bread, all on griddle or iron pot over the turf fire. He taught Denis how to make pancakes. Sometimes he went out at dawn to join his Donnelly cousins whose livelihood was pollan-fishing on Lough Neagh. He came home with plenty for the pan, but he preferred the eels fried in butter and onions that he and Denis caught on their lines. He was invited by the local police sergeant to go duck-shooting along the Bann where game was plentiful, but he declined, apologetically. Eddie came up for a weekend and all the relations and friends from far and wide came at night until the kitchen and loom shop filled up. Anne Donnelly, Tom's first cousin and childhood chum, would recall that 'powerful craic' was enjoyed by all: there were come-all-yees and stories of local scandals and of people 'goin' to law' with neighbours or relatives about a piece

of land or being 'bad-mouthed'. Jimmy McGeown told a riveting tale
of seeing the ghost of The White Lady after midnight near the graveyard
in Derrytrasna – 'It's as true as God's my judge, strike me dead if it's
not!' These nights nearly cleansed his mind.

His leave over, he was given light duties as adjutant to the CO at
the regimental barracks in Belfast: mostly secretarial and liaison work
for the colonel, and explanations of working practices at the Front for
those about to go out there. It was as much as he could cope with. At
his medical examination on 25 March the board reported compassion-
ately: 'His wounds are healed but he has been 3 years and 3 months
at the Front and his nerves are not strong. He cannot concentrate his
attention properly.' Another four months' convalescence was recommended and he was allowed home every ten days for two nights. There
he felt most at ease in the cheerful, undemanding company of Denis.

He could not trouble his mother or Denis with the memories and
thoughts that haunted him, but he shared them with Eddie, who on
several occasions managed an overnight visit to the city. They met at
The Globe and after a pie and a pint took in a film show in the Kinema
or a revue at the Hippodrome, both nearby. A few times they climbed
Cave Hill to the north of the city, making their way to the top through
gentle wooded slopes thickly strewn with bluebells; at the top they
looked down on a smoky industrial city hemmed in by grey shipyards
and black gantries. He was not happy down there.

He kept postponing his planned visit to Bill's mother and wife; it
preyed on his mind for months before he summoned the will to go.
He had difficulties finding Brownlow Street, discovered he had been
given the wrong directions, turned back, and lost heart. In truth, after
Mold he felt he could not look again in the face of inconsolable loss. He
foresaw the wife's hidden resentment, the fatherless child, the mother's
effort to be kind. Perhaps he would go when the War was over. Perhaps
he didn't have to try, because Bill's fate might soon be his too.

It would have been around this time in Belfast, and perhaps at the
request of his family, that the sombre 1918 portrait, showing his MC

ribbon, was taken. Quite unlike the St Omer portrait of the previous year, it seems to show the countenance of a man who has lost all his friends and seen more of killing and maiming than virtually anyone he has ever known.

Tom McAlindon, 1918.

News from the Front did nothing to raise his spirits. From 21 April onwards, even the press could not conceal the successes of the Germans in their last great offensive (or series of offensives). News of the virtual annihilation of the 2nd Battalion at St Quentin cast him into a profound gloom, unable to speak to anyone for days, even at head-quarters. Then the Germans recaptured Messines and Passchendaele

Ridge, were victorious in a third battle of the Aisne, and by 1 June were forty miles from Paris. 'Each one of us must fight to the end,' said Haig in his grim Special Order of the Day, so every month from the hospitals in France 60,000 wounded men were sent back to the Front.

But Allied resistance was stubborn, huge casualties were inflicted on the enemy, and, with the arrival of the Americans, counter-attacks were increasingly successful. Thus although on 15 July the Germans were still expecting peace offers, having Paris at their mercy, on the 23rd the tide of battle turned against them so decisively that the Kaiser announced to his staff: 'I am a defeated Warlord.'

On that very same day, Tom returned to his unit in the trenches near Meteren in Flanders. He had parted from his mother in Derry-loiste with hope renewed and in good spirits; she too was cheerful, believing that this time the War really was near its end, and expecting to see him again soon, which indeed she would. In a hasty note on arrival, he wrote that the fields and orchards in the south of England and in France looked glorious from the train. From time to time the sight of women and children and old men working in the hayfields brought back the very smell of the past and gave him a tremendous yearning for life and normality.

18

About midday on 13 September, Louise and Sadie Stevenson of the Derrytrasna post office were very distressed. A telegram had to be delivered to Mrs Sarah McAlindon of Derryloiste. It said that her son, Captain Thomas McAlindon, was dangerously ill in Fargo Military Hospital at Lark Hill Camp on Salisbury Plain and was asking to see her. It meant, of course, that he was dying: 'Mother' is what all the young men said at the end. The postman had been and gone, and neither of the two sisters wanted to deliver the small yellow envelope, to see the look of fear and dread: every family with a son or husband in the services knew that a telegram meant bad news. Sadie agreed to go and got on her bike; the house was hardly three minutes away. Delivering this message, she would say, was the hardest thing she had ever done.

But it was received with quiet stoicism, the calmness not only of someone who had mentally rehearsed the dread moment many times over, and recently nursed and buried the man who once upon a time she thought she loved; it was the calmness too of a 'handy woman', the district's unofficial, untrained midwife who at all hours of the day and night brought many of the local children into the world. She knew hardship and suffering, life and death, intimately.

Next morning she left Mary Ellen and Annie to look after the cow, the calf and the poultry, and set out on her tortuous journey, taking the eleven-year-old Denis with her for comfort and support. He had been deeply troubled from the start, for she had told them what the telegram really meant. But he knew that for her sake he must be strong and helpful. She had never travelled as far as Belfast, the big city thirty miles away, and at the best of times would have found this journey to the south of England a daunting one. Now it was a journey of sustained anguish. Dressed in her widow's black overcoat, boots and hat, she sat stiffly on the sidecar to Lurgan, silent and withdrawn, holding Denis by the hand. Then there was the train to Belfast, then a sleepless night on the overnight ferry to Liverpool, packed with soldiers returning to the Front; then the long, slow journey by train to London. Worse than these, she told me, was the Underground: she remembered it as a dim and terrible place where tired people stared blankly in front of them as if going to their last end. At the railway stations, Denis asked the questions and got the directions, checked the platform numbers, asked if this or that was the right train. She stood beside him with her purse at the ready and paid for the tickets. Taking the train from Waterloo to Salisbury, they reached Amesbury late that evening and found lodgings. They would catch the bus over to Lark Hill next morning. And the next, and the next.

Tom had arrived by ambulance on the 2nd of the month, the doctors at the base hospital in Le Havre feeling unable to effect any improvement in his deteriorating condition. It was a severe case of enteric (as his medical case sheet termed it) or dysentery. A large proportion of the men at the Front who lined up daily at the MO's sick parade suffered from either constipation or diarrhoea. The first was the result of a diet of hard biscuits and bully beef, and easily treated by the famous 'No. 9 Pill'. The second was a consequence of the unsanitary conditions prevailing in the trenches. Faeces, corpses, dead horses and open or makeshift latrines contaminated everything, especially in the summer months when swarms of flies collected on these and spread infection. In the front line, too, water was often taken at night from streams and shell-holes where the unseen dead were quietly decomposing. The servant assigned to Tom on his return was 'a young fool', he had remarked.

Most cases of diarrhoea never reached a hospital, and spontaneous recovery in a few days was the rule. But before the discovery of antibiotics, those whose symptoms signified bacillary dysentery became distressingly ill and often died. The medical case sheet carefully annotated each day from the 2nd to the 17th of September by Tom's doctor at Fargo Military Hospital makes painful reading. On admission, it says, he was suffering from severe pains in the abdomen, his stools were very frequent, up to twenty per day and consisting mostly of blood and mucus; he had been thus for 8–10 days before admission, and the journey by boat and ambulance has exacerbated his condition. He has a very poor first night at the hospital, with griping pain, and is constantly on the bedpan. All these symptoms persist daily, and on the fifth day he begins to be afflicted by an inflamed back, with boils around his sacrum; on this day, too, the doctor notes for the second time that he is 'very depressed' and will not 'pull himself together'. On the seventh day he develops a severe and constant hiccough and on the tenth his boils get much worse: he is 'still very depressed and takes very little notice'. On the thirteenth day 'he is rather strange in manner and delirious, restless, tries to get out of bed', and 'needs a special watcher'. 'His toxic symptoms are quite intense', his pulse and respiration feeble, and he gets rapidly worse on the fourteenth night. At 9 am on the next day, 17 September, he dies. One outstanding effect of dysentery is not mentioned in the report, perhaps because it is too obvious for comment: emaciation. In a little over three weeks Tom has become a gaunt, hollow-eyed caricature of his handsome self.

There is a suggestion of desperation in Dr Tillman's attempt to save Tom, a consequence no doubt of the limitations of contemporary medicine. He tries albumin water, barley water, bismuth and ricine oil and emetine, starch and opium enemas, salines 'per rectum'. On day three he starts giving brandy every four hours and on day seven puts the patient on champagne, all with no effect on the worsening symptoms. Although his clinical style and his remark on the patient's inability to 'pull himself together' do not reveal it, there may have been compassion as well as desperation in all of this.

Desperation, and a pity beyond telling, were felt by the two people whose stricken presence (understandably) is never alluded to in the doctor's meticulous case sheet. Tom had come through everything – Mons, Neuve Chapelle, the Somme, Ypres, Cambrai; he had been twice wounded and twice returned: and now this. For his mother and for the boy Denis, the nearest thing to a consolation in the whole terrible experience was that once or twice he recognized and spoke to them; but even that was distressing, for his words could not hide at the end the absolute misery, the despair that the doctor called depression.

She told the colonel that she did not want him buried in an English military graveyard, but at home in Derrytrasna, in the graveyard beside the church and the school. He said the army would arrange for the body to be sent over. Then she visited Mr Hedley Bishop, the Amesbury undertaker, carpenter and wheelwright, who said a polished oak coffin would cost £10. A discreet man, he said he thought the regiment would pay for it (it did not) and that he would inquire. He spoke kindly to young Denis, touched him fatherly on the shoulder, and bade them a grave farewell.

She held the boy's hand tightly all the way home, as if afraid of losing him; and they had even less to say to each other than they did when coming over. She kept thinking of the emaciated face and dark sunken eyes, the pathetic corpse, the transformation. Once in 1949 when I sat with her by the open turf fire and had been asking her yet again about Tom, she took her snuff box from her apron pocket and applied a little to each nostril. I knew it had a stinging effect and I asked her why she took the stuff. 'Oh, Tom,' she said, 'it keeps me from thinking.'

On the way back, Denis kept thinking that the doctor's helplessness was his too. He remembered how he could save Tom from his terrors in the night with gentle words and a reassuring touch, but now he knew his brother was in the grip of some malignant thing bent on total supremacy. He thought bitterly too on the war that was to end all wars and to end before Christmas, that wounded Tom and wounded him again and then poisoned and maddened and killed him with its stinking trenches. Once it was a great mystery to him; exciting. Now he feared and hated it as men lost in the jungle fear and hate the trackless vast they know they will die in.

Like its myriad lookalikes in Belgium and France, Tom's headstone is of austere and classical simplicity, installed and still cared for by the Commonwealth War Graves Commission. A few paces from the High Road on which he went forth so cheerfully in 1908, it stands out in marked isolation from the headstones of all those who lived out their quiet lives in Derryinver, Derrytrasna and Derryloiste.

PART TWO

World War II
The Burmese Jungle

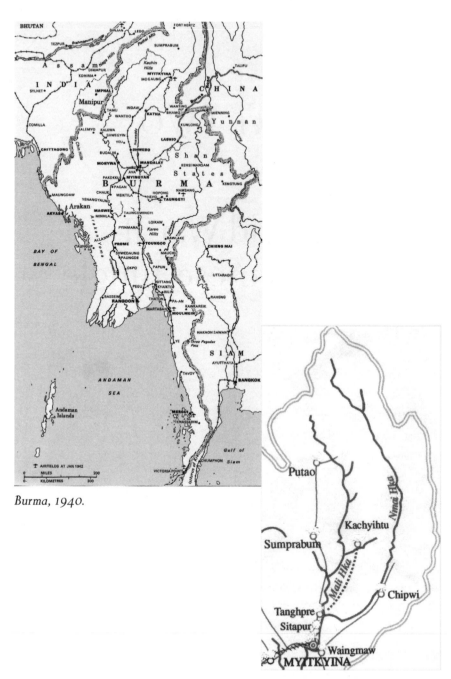

Burma, 1940.

The Myitkyina area, northern Burma, 1940. Courtesy of the Missionary Society of St Columban.

19

In 1921 Eddie left the Royal Irish Constabulary, found employment in Belfast, and within three years, being still unmarried, was able to meet Denis's fees as a boarder in St Colman's College, Newry. Tom had told the boy that a secondary education was the passport to a quick commission in the army, but although he shared Tom's desire to see the wider world, his brother's wounds and nightmares, and the memory of his sunken eyes and skeletal frame, left him with no desire to become a soldier. His inclination, born in part of that terrible experience at Lark Hill, was to save lives. For financial reasons, a medical career was obviously out of the question; yet his inclination to save people would be fulfilled in various ways, not all of them predictable.

A common feature of life in Catholic colleges such as St Colman's was visits from members of religious orders and societies soliciting vocations to the priesthood, either monastic or missionary: these men were the religious equivalents of army recruiting sergeants, and usually far more eloquent. A priest from the Missionary Society of St Columban, which was working at that time in China, urged his young hearers to think of devoting their lives to what he termed the noblest work on earth, the extension of the kingdom of Jesus Christ throughout the world. A priest, he said, was a man chosen by Christ to take His place on earth and to complete His work, the salvation of immortal souls. No other office or profession, however great or exalted, could compare with the priesthood. A thousand million pagans waited to be saved by priests willing to venture into distant lands and endure hardship for the highest of causes.

Exhortations such as these, illustrated with descriptions of the hazardous journeys and tough but rewarding work undertaken by the Society's members in remote territories, appealed to the idealism of youth and, vaguely but powerfully, to their sense of adventure, their attraction to the dangerous unknown. The world has hugely contracted since then, and it is almost impossible now to appreciate the glamour that 'faraway places' held for young people whose lives were intensely constricted by comparison with what is the norm today.

Towards the end of his final year at St Colman's, Denis answered the call to become a missionary priest and duly applied for admission. The full implications of lifelong celibacy were perhaps never fully apparent to youths such as Denis when they decided to become priests. But the choice was accepted as intrinsic to the notion of self-sacrifice in total commitment to the higher cause. And besides, what Denis had seen of married life would not have made it figure in his mind as the one and only path to personal fulfilment and happiness.

However urgent its appeals for new members, the Columban Society was exacting in its admission procedures and wanted healthy young men of sound character and good intelligence. Denis was an ideal candidate. The president of St Colman's warmly supported his application to the Society, saying that four years in the college had shown him to be 'a splendid character, pious, obedient, industrious in any work in which he is engaged, and gifted with brains beyond the average'. His former parish priest, now Canon O'Hagan of St Peter's in Lurgan, wrote that 'a better student and young man is not to be found in any college in Ireland': a large claim, but one which the Society's members many years later would endorse when they elected him their vicar general for an unprecedentedly long period.

In 1927 he donned clerical black and entered the Society's college in Galway to begin his six years' preparation for the priesthood. Like Tom's six-year induction to actual warfare, it was systematic, intense and demanding, and placed great emphasis on self-discipline. But there was no harshness: the ideal of behaviour held up to the young men, practised as well as preached by their superiors (all of them demo-cratically elected to higher office for limited periods), was Christlike gentleness and fraternal kindliness, qualities of special importance to men working together in small groups or pairs in remote places and difficult circumstances. The primary focus of the six years' preparation was theological study, but manual labour on the college's farm and the development of practical skills such as would be imperative in mission-ary conditions were part of the daily routine. And in fact an outstanding feature of Denis's character, due in large measure to the nature of his home life, was a tough and practical versatility. It was said that 'he could turn his hand to anything'.

His exceptional intelligence, however, was apparent to his superi-ors, and after his ordination he was sent to take a postgraduate degree in theology at the Gregorian University in Rome. As it turned out, this refinement and extension of what he had already been taught was of no value whatever in the life he would soon be leading. Two years in Rome, with all its history and culture, was of course immensely exciting in itself, a great broadening of the mind, but a concentrated course in med-icine and other survival skills would have been much more appropriate than advanced theology for what lay ahead. Yet in the course of his life as a missionary, he would acquire a remarkable knowledge, both theoreti-cal and practical, of medical matters. In rough circumstances abroad, he became of necessity a self-taught amateur doctor, much as his mother became unofficial midwife to all her neighbours in the Montiaghs.

By the time of his return from Rome in 1936, the Society was expanding rapidly and operating in Korea, the Philippines and Indone-sia, as well as China. It was now being asked by the relevant authority in Rome – the Congregation of Propaganda Fide ('Propaganda' for short)

– to send missionaries to a mountainous jungle region in the far north of Burma. Until 1928 this area was designated by the British colonial government as 'Unadministered Territory', a dangerous area where the Nagas in the west engaged in headhunting and human sacrifice and the Kachins in the east in routine kidnapping and slavery. It was a part of Burma that the Burmese themselves – a racially distinct group altogether – avoided as hostile and fearful. Historically, relations between them and the various peoples of the north, the Karens and Kachins especially, had always been conflictual.

Denis McAlindon. Ordination photo, 1933.

Like the Baptist missionaries who had been working in Burma for many years, Rome recognized that the northern peoples would find Christian belief much more attractive than would the Burmese. They were animists and believed they were subject in their daily lives to capricious spirits – the *nats* – who caused illness and misfortune and required costly rituals of propitiation. The Burmese by contrast had embraced the gentle doctrines of the Buddha and had found them so entirely satisfying that Buddhist and Burmese became almost synonymous terms — to abandon Buddhism was to cease to be Burmese.

Obviously, the British administration looked favourably on Christian missionary work in the north, seeing it as reinforcing their attempts to introduce law and order to that wild region. By 1936 they had largely eliminated headhunting in the Unadministered Territory, emancipated over 9000 slaves, compensated their owners, and introduced a system of local government, with elected village headmen responsible to the central government. A road had been opened up between Bhamo, the Kachin state capital, and Fort Hertz (also called Putao) in the far north. This new administrative outpost was situated in the beautiful Golden Plain, bordering on Tibet and in sight of the snow-capped Himalayas – a noted wonderland for botanists.

The adventurous idealism that inspired the young Irish missionaries who set out for northern Burma in 1936 had many established models. There was the Apostle Paul, who preached Christian monotheism to the worshippers of Greek and Roman deities in all the countries and communities of the Mediterranean and the Aegean, and the Apostle Thomas, reputed to have travelled to India and founded the Christian church there. There were more recent saints such as Francis of Assisi and Ignatius Loyola, young knights who consciously converted their initial pursuit of military glory into spiritual chivalry and warfare – saving lost souls, destroying idols, combating the powers of the devil in its worldly incarnations; for them, the military ideal became a metaphor for active Christianity. The lives of the saints were standard reading at mealtimes in the refectories of clerical colleges and enhanced the feeling of intending missionaries that they were embarking on a great spiritual adventure that had been going on uninterruptedly since the time of Christ and His Apostles.

20

Apart from a two-week course on tropical diseases at University College Dublin, Denis and his five companions chosen to go to Burma were given no special preparation. As well as the necessaries for saying Mass, they were equipped with a medical handbook and a compact medicine chest, on the correct assumption that by ministering to ailing bodies they would be the more welcome as saviours of the soul.

There was no collective ceremony to mark their departures. As quietly as medieval pilgrims, each of them bade farewell to his family and left for Burma from his own home. Denis's mother and his sister Mary Ellen walked with him to meet the Lurgan bus at the crossroads (the sidecar by now a thing of the past), and the Stevenson sisters, less agile than when Tom left, emerged from the post office to wish him well. There was pride and hope as well as some sadness in the embraces of his mother and sister. 'God willing,' he said, 'I'll be home for extended leave in three or four years. The time will fly.' He took a seat at the back of the bus and watched and waved until a dip in the High Road hid them from view.

He met the rest of the group in the port of Dublin on board the SS *Domala*, an ancient creaky vessel, half-cargo and half-passenger. They travelled via London (where engine trouble caused a 48-hour delay) to Calcutta, and from Calcutta to Rangoon; this journey lasted six weeks and two days and gave them time to acquire a sense of distance and to observe the realities of cultural difference and historical change.

The old steamer stopped for a few days ('from fatigue', said Denis) at various ports en route. First there was Malta, where they visited St Paul's Bay, hallowed by tradition as the inlet where the intrepid Apostle was shipwrecked and came ashore (Acts 27–8); here too they heard much from their guide about the famous Knights of Malta, men who combined the religious and the military life, being sworn in holy orders to poverty, celibacy and obedience, and dedicated to defending Christendom against the Muslim invaders to whose powerful advances much of eastern Europe and north Africa had fallen in the sixteenth century.

They stopped at Port Said and began their adjustment to their new life at the legendary Simon Artz's store, purchasing tropical attire and discarding their clerical black for years to come. They stopped for a night and a day at Suez, whose great canal had facilitated European colonization of Africa and, since 1869, been a source of colonial rivalry between the French and the British – a contest which ended coincidentally at the time of the priests' visit in 1936 when the British secured official control of the waterway. They stopped at Aden, where a tout-cum-guide who told them he had seven wives gave them their first acquaintance with Islam.

They stopped at Colombo, whose great natural harbour attracted Romans, Arabs and Chinese traders long before the Portuguese seized and christianized it in the sixteenth century, the Dutch in the seventeenth, and the British in the eighteenth (later making it the capital of their Crown colony, Ceylon). Then they rounded into the Bay of Bengal and stopped at Vizag, where the names of primary and secondary schools such as Stella Maris, St Joseph's, St Francis De Sales's and St Ann's testified to the tolerance or quiescence of the native Hindus as well as the energy of the Christians. At Madras they visited Mylapore and the Cathedral of San Thomé, built by the Portuguese in the sixteenth century. 'It would have been imprudent' (wrote Denis with character-istic irony many years later in an account of this journey) 'to deny that the church held the tomb of St Thomas the Apostle.' It would have been even more imprudent to question whether the doubting Apostle had ever been to India, a claim dismissed by Hindu historians as an attempt to present Christianity as an indigenous Indian religion rather than a Western import. Material and spiritual conquest; merchants, soldiers and holy men; commerce, domination and persuasion; history, legend and propaganda: for those of them who had eyes to see, the nature of the human world was unfolding before them like a mazy oriental carpet.

They reached Rangoon on 26 November and were met by Father Pat Donohue, a very friendly priest who was a great help in showing them the city and booking their passage to Mandalay some 300 miles north. A man with a most intriguing history, he appeared in all physi-cal respects Indian – South Indian or Tamil – 'But,' remarked Denis in his usual style, 'he may have had somewhere an Irish ancestor.' He was born in Burma, became a doctor, and served with the British army on the Western Front. On being disbanded in London, he heard about the new mission to China and offered his medical services there. When his brother, a priest in southern Burma, died, he left China, studied for the priesthood himself and was now ministering in the Rangoon area. With Indian Pat, Denis felt a strange and deep affinity. He envied his medical expertise (and was most grateful for the gift of some medical textbooks). There was much he would have liked to talk to him about in private and was sorry when they parted. For Pat's past was Tom's too, and he prompted in Denis the thought that with just a little more luck his brother could have been enjoying life as a peacetime soldier here in Burma or in another of those distant countries painted bright by the old fusilier and promised by Sergeant Major O'Toole.

From Mandalay they travelled by train north to Katha and then by riverboat on the great Irrawaddy eastward to Bhamo. These were long journeys, Burma being almost as big as England and France com-bined, 1200 miles long from south to north. Bhamo was one of the two civil districts comprising the Kachin state, the other being Myitkyina, further north. After the heat and dust and congestion of the train, the river journey was delightful. Father Pat had booked them places on the top deck of one of the Irrawaddy Flotilla Company's paddle steamers, all Clyde-built, and this one, the *Annie Laurie*, with a Scottish captain. Under a roof on the top deck, they sat at the bow's edge on deckchairs and enjoyed the breezes and the passing scene, with meals and drinks served by polite Indian waiters in immaculate white: a pleasurable and, for them, unique but slightly disturbing experience of colonial ease and elegance. While the people on the lower deck squatted on their bundles and kept their chickens in order, they watched strange river birds swooping round and about, caught sight of golden deer drinking shyly on little sandy beaches, and from time to time waved back to riverside children for whom the passing of the great vessel was a special wonder. Halfway to Bhamo they were startled out of reverie when it seemed as if the steamer was heading straight for a gigantic cliff; but then it moved slightly to the right and entered a gorge about 250 yards wide, following for several miles a winding course below towering, vertical cliffs on either side. This was the famous Second Defile, a fitting gateway to the darker side of Burma.

Thanks to Father Jim Stuart, the chattiest member of the group, they fell into conversation after this with an agreeable Englishman, Mr Leslie, an Oxford graduate and administrative officer in the Indian Civil Service. He was returning from leave and on his way back to his post in the Kachin hills, close to the border with China; he was looking forward not only to his work as magistrate but also to indulging the passions he had brought with him from England – hunting, fishing and lepidoptera (his collection, he said, was still far short of the 350 specimens found in the country). He was a contented bachelor and said he quite enjoyed his solitude in the hills: not that he could be called a true solitary, since he had a Punjabi policeman, a Kachin cook and three Karen clerks-cum-translators all living in his compound. He told the priests that when he had passed his entrance examination for the ICS he had made Burma, then a province of the Indian empire, his first choice, even though the most ambitious candidates always chose India; he chose Burma for 'the simple and silly reason that it sounded romantic'. But like most of his colleagues in Burma, he loved the country and had never regretted his choice. He was quietly proud of the British empire and believed that British rule in India and Burma was largely benevolent. 'And what about Ireland?' asked Jim Stuart with a smile. 'Ah well, that's undoubtedly another story,' he conceded. But on the subject of imperialism, he reminded them that the history of the world was the history of strong tribes expelling or dominating weak ones; battles in which the winners take the prizes; the viceroy was just the last of a long line of conquerors in India and Burma. The point to remember was that some conquerors and their laws and customs were a lot more beneficent to the natives than those they displaced. When the English took over in Burma in 1886, they expelled a king called Thibaw. On his succession in 1878, the delectable Thibaw had seventy-nine of his relatives — men, women and children — put to death in the so-called Massacre of the Kinsmen. That was the customary right of any new monarch who happened to feel insecure on his throne. 'Some custom.'

'Anyhow,' Mr Leslie added slyly, 'what about you chaps? Don't you depend on us imperialists, however indirectly? And don't you assume — rightly no doubt — that you are about to improve the lives and beliefs of tribesmen who never asked you to come? Are you not spiritual imperialists?' And later he added: 'But on the matter of dependence and all that, when you're settled in Bhamo you must get in contact with Robin McGuire — he's due for a move but should still be there. District Commissioner. A fine chap. A compatriot of yours.'

21

The DC in Bhamo had at his back a battalion of the Frontier Force. These were semi-military police and a reminder that this town, a settlement with an estimated population of 6000, was a frontier post; it was still rather primitive, located at the edge of the recently tamed northern hills and hardly fifty miles from the Chinese border. But it was a popular assignment for British administrators, a colourful place swarming with a diversity of physical types and tribal costumes; in its buzzing bazaar, as well as some Burmese, they saw Indians of various kinds, Chinese (Yunanese, Cantonese), Kachins, Karens, Nagas and Shans, all chattering in their own languages with their own people and bartering with others in what they knew of Burmese, the *lingua franca*. Denis nicknamed it 'Babel' – affectionately, for he had a fascination with languages satisfied so far only in the mastery of Italian he had acquired in Rome.

But at first the charm of which their travelling companion had spoken was not apparent to the other young missionaries, and there were constraints on what Mr McGuire could do for them. The priests from the Paris Foreign Mission, who were vacating the district, had left at their disposal the Clergy House, a wooden-frame building raised on posts with dilapidated bamboo matting for walls, the lower part recently enclosed to provide a store room. They squeezed into this building as best they could, above and below, and settled down to plan their future. Their first task was to learn Kachin, which they found relatively easy, especially because of the friendliness of Kachin schoolboys and the fact that its first and only written form was in Roman script (the work of an admirable nineteenth-century Baptist missionary). Burmese was much more difficult for them to learn; Denis studied it under the tutelage of a Shan boy who, he remarked, knew little English and not too much Burmese.

Because of the strong Baptist presence in the town, the Columbans were not allowed to seek new converts. They confined themselves instead to ministering to the needs of existing Catholics, most of them located in villages scattered around the Kachin hills to the east and south-east of Bhamo. Looking for a zone of their own where the administration would allow them to undertake active missionary work, they set their sights on the Triangle; this was an area between the Nmai and the Mali, two rivers that joined – at the so-called 'Confluence' – to form the Irrawaddy, twenty-seven miles north of Myitkyina. A mountainous jungle tract reaching the borders of Tibet, ninety miles long and forty at its widest point, the Triangle was still unmapped territory and deemed unsafe by the British; they were aware that their pacifying activities of 1927 had left some bitterness among the tribesmen. It had a widely scattered population of over 60,000, the majority of them Kachin, the remainder comprising six or seven other distinct racial and linguistic groups.

With admission to the Triangle in view, in June 1938 Jim Stuart and Denis moved up to Myitkyina, the most northerly of the administrative towns. Although they confined themselves to working with the few Catholics in the Myitkyina district, their presence was contested by the Baptists, who argued that it could only confuse the Kachins, that there had already been friction between Baptist and Catholic Kachins in Bhamo, and that they alone should be allowed to evangelize and teach in the area. At first, the administration seemed to agree and was anxious

to avoid sectarian squabbling. It would not give a good impression of
the white man.

Twenty years later, after Jim's death, Denis put on record an account
of the way in which both the administration and the Baptists were won
round to an acceptance of their presence and their entry into the Triangle. Characteristically, he said nothing whatever about himself in this
memoir ('Fr Jim Stuart: a Great Missionary', *The Far East*, November
1955, pp. 7–15); instead, he emphasized Jim's easy, sociable nature and
the way in which he managed to break down prejudice, meeting the
British officials in their offices, clubs and homes, talking and making
friends with them, and gradually gaining the goodwill of the Baptists.
One can reasonably assume that Denis's own quiet diplomacy and good
humour played its part in all of this.

Permission to enter the Triangle was secured in 1939, and on 26
March Denis and Jim set out on a journey of exploration: their goal,
a site suitable for a mission house, a church and a school – a station
that would form the centre of their missionary activities in the whole
region. (In his 1962 account of this journey, a document found in the
Columban Fathers' archives in Navan and originally written in response
to queries from America about Father Stuart's work in Burma, Denis
again made no mention of himself but wrote as if Jim travelled alone.)
They set out on foot carrying the bare necessities – Mass kit, food,
cooking utensils and a thin bedroll. They had of course no maps and
only a hazy idea of the geography of the place; even the names of the
villages were unknown to them. The dialect too (Hkahku) was strange
at first; many words for ordinary things were different from the Kachin
they had learned in Bhamo.

The villagers they encountered were cautious at first but then
friendly and inquisitive. At one village, Wagarawt, a pagan festival and
sacrifice were in progress when they arrived. On a great altar at the
edge of the village a cow had been slaughtered (as the headman later
explained) to make peace with an angry *nat* who had caused the rice
famine that was making them all so hungry. The meat would be consumed

by the villagers, and the *nat* would be satisfied with its life. Of course the priests knew about the animistic beliefs of the Kachins but refrained at this point from observing that in spite of the feast the sacrificial practice was not in the long run materially beneficial to the people. They simply observed that in their own religion when human beings were genuinely at fault, confesssing and being truly sorry for one's sins would bring forgiveness from the Creator of the world. The headman seemed interested in this view of the way in which the supernatural and the natural orders related, but he was much more interested in their declared intention to start a school. His people were very poor, he said, and if their sons could read and write, the government would give them work, or they could join the army. A Kachin who spoke the government's language had already been given government work and a wooden house further to the north, and plenty of Kachins living in and near Bhamo who knew a little English were now in the military police or the army.

It was clear to the priests that the headman knew nothing about their religion and had no word for 'priest'. But the word 'school' he knew well, and he almost demanded that they stay and build one. They tried to explain that wherever they built their school his children could come and stay there as boarders. He in turn explained that the children could not be away from the village during the dry months when trees were being cut down and burned and the ground prepared for planting vegetables and rice – they never used the same area for cultivation more than once in twelve years. He explained that everyone had to be involved in this demanding work. It was dangerous work too, for sometimes they could unintentionally disturb a tiger's lair. His wife's brother had been about to leave a new place one evening when a tiger went for him. Did he escape? Yes, he climbed a tree and when the tiger refused to go away, he kept shouting at it, saying, 'Why are you threatening me? There never has been any trouble between your people and mine!' It went away. The priests were uncertain whether the headman was naïve or a deadpan humorist who thought his visitors as simple-minded as his brother-in-law.

Of the half-dozen or so bamboo houses in Wagarawat (all built on stilts), the headman's was the longest; he allowed the priests to cook their rice and sleep in one of the differentiated spaces or *daps* (there were no partitioned rooms). Politely they waited until he had prepared his nightly opium 'fix', which he did with elaborate ceremony, and then withdrew. Exhausted after their day's slogging and their linguistic efforts, they spread their bedrolls on the bamboo floor and fell promptly asleep, only briefly distracted by the grunting of pigs below them and the snoring of the headman, his wife, his brothers and their wives. In the morning, the whole village assembled to bid them goodbye; they saw in the smiles and excitement of the children who jostled about them an intimation of the future they had come to shape.

For a week they followed the villagers' paths up and down one jungly hill after another, wading waist-deep or rock-hopping across lively streams, and trying with minimum success to steer due north. Sometimes they slept in the remains of an abandoned village, mostly in others like Wagarawt where they met the same kind of reception. Most of the villages were perched on almost inaccessible hill-slopes, accessed by a long wooded entrance, which provided substantial evidence of the religion they had come to eradicate. There were posts with crude pictures of grain, weapons and other things which, as they would learn in time, the people wanted the *nats* to give them. There were little bamboo shrines with offerings for the *nats*, a chicken or a jar of *zu*, the local liquor; and sometimes across the path was strung a line on which were hanging numerous star-shaped ornaments made of bamboo intended to keep off the *nats* that caused cholera, small pox, goitre and cattle disease.

By the end of a week, they had seen nothing like a suitable space for a mission compound. Moreover, their rice was running out, and because of the current blight the people had none to sell them. Inexperience and enthusiasm had left them in desperate straits and could easily have had fatal consequences. They turned back and on their way subsisted on fish caught with forked sticks in the shallower streams and some sweet potatoes found growing near a derelict village. Jim grew feverous, shivering constantly; he was clearly suffering from malaria when they got back to Myitkyina on 6 April. Both men were exhausted, and Denis was extremely hungry. They realized that much more travelling, with better equipment and supplies, would have to be done before an acceptable site could be found.

A second and a third journey of exploration were made, Jim travelling on these occasions with other members of the group now in Myitkyina, Denis staying behind to take charge of planning and supplies. They travelled by way of Sumprabum, a small government hill station more than 130 miles north of Myitkyina. Ponies were used for transport, with mules carrying provisions sufficient for several months. The road to Sumprabum followed the Mali River gorge for fifty miles or so; it then plunged westwards through wild mountainous country along a sequence of huge canyons dense with tangled green jungle. Looking down into that yawning wilderness, it was easy for the travellers to understand Kachin belief in Nature's malevolent and unpredictable spirits.

Then they crossed the Sinan and Mali Rivers by raft. On the third journey, the Mali had risen to dangerous heights and they were delayed for two days at a riverside village; this kind of delay, the missionaries would find, was a common experience for travellers in the region. Once across, they struck eastwards into the hills. The mosquitoes made the nights miserable, and the blood-sucking leeches were a daily torment. They removed the leeches with the lighted end of a cigarette but often failed to see that they had made their way into their shoes, so that at night they would find their socks saturated in blood.

By this time, World War II had begun in Europe. They had heard about it before the second trip began, but now it seemed an utterly distant event, with no relevance or connection whatever to what they were doing and where they were going. In the latter assumption, as time would soon tell, they were wrong. But for the moment, let us stay with them in their time of peace and their search for a suitable place.

22

The name of the suitable place was Kajihtu, a tiny village some forty miles east of Sumprabum, 3500 feet up in the hills. Its discovery, after tortuous climbing through torrential rains and after many mishaps, cost the life of one priest, John Dunlea, and brought Patrick Ussher, the group's superior in Bhamo, close to death. Both of them were the victims of typhoid; Jim Stuart had a milder attack of the same and returned in very poor shape to Myitkyina. By the time the explorers had settled on Kajihtu, the difficulties and dangers of living and moving about in this region were fully apparent.

At Kajihtu they were lucky to encounter an English- and Burmese-speaking Kachin, La Doi. He had been many years in government service and was now the official *Taung-ok* or native over-chief of the village headmen in the Southern Triangle, selected for his ability and his knowledge of Kachin customs. He agreed with the priests that this village would be an ideal site for a mission station and a school, and he persuaded the elders to gift them some land beside the village. When cleared by the villagers of trees, it looked perfect for the purpose. Father Ussher gave it his whole-hearted approval. Set in a great amphitheatre of steep mountain ranges sloping westwards, it consisted of fifteen acres covering the entire summit of a well-rounded hill. It had level spaces for buildings, a playground and a vegetable garden, and two streams of cool fresh water gushing from the rocks through moss and ferns. On a clear day, one could glimpse the white glitter of the Himalayas beyond the surrounding hills and canyons. It seemed at times a place of rare beauty.

The mission station at Kajihtu, c.2000. Courtesy of Father Owen O'Leary.

It would be Denis and Jim's station, with Denis as the anchor man, for unforeseen circumstances would send Jim far afield for long periods; and eventually Denis would be its sole occupant. Fully equipped, in December 1940 the two set out for the village from Myitkyina. They chose not to travel by Sumprabum, but by the more direct though more difficult route, crossing the Irrawaddy just north of the Confluence, thirty-two miles above Myitkyina. They were prepared to start building as soon as they arrived, but their progress was slow. Every nail, screw, saw, chisel, hammer, screwdriver and hand-drill had to be carried on mules, whose sure but stubbornly slow pace determined the rate of progress: it took them almost four weeks.

The villagers had been impatient for their arrival and held a party to celebrate the occasion. Next morning the priests set up a makeshift sawpit to begin building their wooden mission house, only to discover that sawyers and carpenters were unknown in the Triangle: bamboo and bamboo strapping and a good *dah* (dagger) were all that was needed for building native homes and rafts: a large abode could be erected in a day or two at most, all the villagers lending a hand. After a delay that sorely tested the patience of the priests, two sawyers were located in the Fort Hertz (Putao) area and a carpenter was fetched from Sumprabum. Eventually, a two-storied wooden building was erected, the lower part divided into schoolrooms and the upper part between a church and living accommodation. Bamboo buildings were erected to accommodate the boarders who would come from the surrounding villages. Then from Bhamo were recruited two teachers, Mwa and Lazing Tu, the second of whom undertook to buy and store rice for the little community at a village along the Irrawaddy. And at last, with a sense of achievement and exhilaration on the part of Denis and Jim, and much music and dancing and dressing-up on that of the villagers, the school was opened in May (1940). It was named St Mary's Mission School, May being the month devoted to the Virgin Mary.

Winning converts to their faith would not be quite so straightforward as building a wooden church. But fortuitously the government began the first-ever census of the hill territories in February and March and asked the two priests to take charge of it in the Triangle. Rendering service to Caesar in this way gave them a perfect opportunity to make themselves known to everyone in the area, to account for their presence, and, when the opportunity arose, to explain the basics of the Roman Catholic faith and their view of the *nats*. While building proceeded at Kajihtu, with La Doi keeping an eye on developments, they travelled for six weeks from village to village with a guide and a catechist, the latter a young Catholic Kachin from Bhamo who had been several years in the army. Usually when it came to talking about the *nats* the catechist would eagerly take over and tell the family how foolish he himself had been to believe that fevers and ulcers and goitre and bad crops were caused by evil spirits; he said that trying to propitiate these imaginary spirits with eggs and poultry and farm animals had made the Kachins a poor people. The *jau du ni* (the priests) had medicines that could cure most of these illnesses and could teach them about kind spirits, called angels and saints, and a good god who ruled over all. When he first delivered this apologia, the catechist was suddenly embarrassed, having intervened spontaneously, but Denis and Jim, although amused, perceived its value and always encouraged it.

At each village the pattern repeated itself. People were pleased to answer questions about ages and relationships and family history and to add much that was not quite relevant to the census: information about the wickedest man in the valley and how many had been killed in fights with the Nagas and the sub-tribes and with the British when they came to stop raiding and slavery. Often they disclosed that some of those presently alive in the village had been slaves and stayed on and married a Kachin, or were the children of slaves. The census interview turned into a little ritual that the people enjoyed, the children ringed round in attentive silence, absorbing their communal history.

When the priests and the catechist had talked about their mission, the priests would say that if any of the villagers decided to have the *nats* thrown out they should send a message to Kajihtu and one of them would return to do so and to instruct them in the Catholic faith. If their children came to the school they would be taught the Catholic catechism as a matter of course. There was no rush to embrace the faith, but much interest in the medicines and the school. As for reactions to the Good News, Denis was at first reminded of what the Corinthians said to St Paul: 'We will hear thee again' – i.e., 'Some other time'.

But 1941 was a year of success. The children settled in quickly, were attentive and easy to teach, and their singing and their cries at playtime brought a new joy to the hills. Denis planted a large vegetable garden that quickly sprouted and on which they would rely heavily for their curries in years to come; he relished this work, having acquired green fingers in the family garden in Derryloiste. The 'mustard seed' of faith too (a favourite biblical metaphor with missionaries) had begun to germinate in the hills. The Kajihtu headman was the first to ask for his family's altar to be destroyed and the *nats* thrown out. Others in the village began to follow his example, and every other week the catechist would return with requests from a family or families in outlying villages. The priest would dismantle and burn the altar and the images, set up his own altar of bamboo, adorned with a picture of the Virgin Mary and the Sacred Heart, and then say Mass.

A pastoral programme, involving a week's journeying from village to village, gradually evolved:

We have settled in to a nice routine by now [he wrote to his mother on 29 November]. I usually set off early on Monday morning, with a porter to help with my luggage – Mass kit, bed-roll, medicines, tiffin holder (a handy three-decker instrument carrying cooked meals, normally rice and curry). The going is slow and we would arrive at the village towards evening. A meal is ready for us, and my bed-roll is taken and spread out on the bamboo floor close to the fire in the place of honour. I am happy to bed down early, for next day will be full and busy. First thing in the morning I hear confessions, then I say Mass, which the whole village, the pagans as well as the converts, usually attends. I give a little sermon on the Good News, and after Mass the catechist brings forward those whom he has prepared for baptism; those who pass the examination are duly given the sacrament. The people all gather round; they seem to love the simple solemnity of our rituals.

Afterwards there is a celebratory meal to which all the villagers, and those from outlying homes, contribute – in the morning or the night before, they bring live chickens with their legs tied together, eggs secured in bamboo containers, rice and tomatoes and tsabee, the native beer, and sometimes everyone contributes to the purchase of a small pig for a curry.

After the meal, there are the sick to attend to and the medicines to be distributed: aspirin or 'sweat medicine' for fever, quinine for malaria, tincture of iodine or 'swollen neck medicine' for goitre (very common here among girls and women), liquid iodine and antiseptic ointment for cuts, bruised feet, ulcers etc. The patients usually bring payment in kind, a chicken, eggs, vegetables, rice.

If it has been a particularly auspicious day (conversion of a headman or one of the elders or a whole family) sports will follow: games, dancing, and music. One of their favourite games is 'Hit the bucket': senior members of the community are blindfolded, given a stick, and sent in search of the bucket. Their stumbling efforts cause great hilarity, especially among the women, who themselves always refuse to participate and lose face. Their dancing is a kind of Follow My Leader, the first person dictating the pattern of movement for the chain of people attached to him; the headman leads off, the women follow, then the children, and drums, gongs and cymbals beat out the rhythm. On these occasions I'm usually persuaded to postpone our departure until the next morning. And so on to the next village, and the next, and the next, arriving back at Kajihtu on Friday afternoon.

The Kajihtans are all glad to see us return from our respective trips and they seem to trust us, for they have begun to ask our advice on village disputes as well as medical matters. Friday evening is our favourite time. Jim and I compare notes on our trips and relax on the verandah with tired feet up and a pot of tea and take in the marvellous skyline at sunset. In the morning the mountain ridges emerge slowly from heavy mists, but in the evening they are sharply etched in all their various formations against the sky, and magically coloured in ever-changing hues. Then the dark falls suddenly and early, the way it always does in the tropics. But there is a marvellous canopy of glittering stars, the like of which we never see at home; the ceiling of the Sistine Chapel that I got *to know so well seems tawdry by comparison. I know we are doing good here and sometimes feel I could stay in Kajihtu forever.*

In September Jim set off with three carriers for Myitkyina and Bhamo and was away for over a month. He was stocking up on medicine and food and reporting to Father Ussher on progress in the Triangle; he was also making the census returns and nurturing good relations with the administrative officers – 'Rendering to Caesar and all that,' he would say. This was likely to become a twice- or thrice-yearly trip.

The year 1941 ended with the first Christmas ever to be celebrated in the Triangle, bringing for the two priests a profound sense of achievement and spiritual satisfaction. They felt as if they were back in the first century AD creating the first Christian community, bringing light and comfort to a people enslaved to vindictive spirits, converting to a doctrine of peace tribesmen hitherto known only for their slave raids and their warlike propensities. With neither newspaper nor radio to distract them, they were cut off from the world outside, firmly rooted in their own. Europe was now deep in its old turmoil, but the demanding fullness of their spiritual and humanitarian routine made that seem more remote than ever.

Unknown to them, however, on 7 December the Japanese, with shocking suddenness, had attacked and destroyed the US fleet in Pearl Harbour and proceeded thus to extend the European conflict to the Far East; the Crown Colony of Hong Kong fell to them on Christmas Day. They would bring World War II to the Kachin hills before June 1942, and Denis's mother would soon be writing desperate letters to the Society's superior general, asking if anything had been heard of her son: fearful lest she would lose him to this war as she had lost Tom to the last.

In less than six months, the invaders drove the British, the Americans and the Dutch out of all their south-east Asian possessions, one of the most staggering feats in military history. The supposedly impregnable British fortress of Singapore fell to them in February, and the invasion of Burma followed. Rangoon was taken on 8 March, Lashio on 26 April, Bhamo and Myitkyina on 7 May. Mandalay had been virtually destroyed from the air on 3 April, 2000 of its inhabitants being killed in the raids; it was occupied on 1 May. After taking Myitkyina, the Japanese army came to a halt but sent a patrol up through Sumprabum towards Fort Hertz, a thousand miles from Rangoon. They narrowly missed Kajihtu, inconveniently placed as it was in roadless hills forty miles to the right. Since the monsoon was upon them, the road and tracks impassable, and their supplies exhausted, the patrol turned back at the end of May, abandoning their plan to establish themselves in Fort Hertz. The army encamped below Sumprabum, but not before warning everyone in that little town that they would return in the dry season.

The British and Chinese armies had fought desperate rearguard actions to avoid encirclement and make their escape from the country: the British went north-west into India, the Chinese due north via the Hukwang valley or Fort Hertz and thence into Tibet and China. Most of the Burmese members of the British regiments were disinclined to fight against the Japanese, who came as self-styled liberators of their country; they just drifted away and in many cases acted as spies for the enemy. The Shans, Karens and Kachins, who had always felt safer with the British than with the Burmese, remained loyal to them. The British administration took charge of 400,000 civilian evacuees, both British and Indians, including women and children, all desperate to escape the ruthless invader. The latter stage of this retreat was on foot through malarial hills on the Indian border; 10,000 died on the way. How many thousand Chinese soldiers perished is not known, but every track in the Hukwang valley and the Kachin hills was littered with their rotting bodies before the monsoon ended.

On 25 March 1942, Father Stuart, ignorant of what was going on elsewhere in the country, made what he thought was another routine trip to Myitkyina, only to encounter shocking evidence of the unfolding disaster. The place was in total disorder. Thieving deserters and thousands of refugees from Rangoon, hungry and exhausted, were all milling around; no one knew what to do or where to go. Of transport and food there was none; the last plane had just left from a hurriedly constructed airstrip, carrying the Governor General and his entourage. Heading back to Kajihtu via Sumprabum, Jim found the situation in that town equally bad. Here, too, he was abruptly caught up in the refugee crisis himself: a Mr Stevenson, probably the last British official to flee from Burma, pleaded with him to take charge of a band of orphans from a Church of England school in Rangoon. He agreed to do so. Many of the children, suffering from starvation, exhaustion and fever, died while in his care; these he buried, but – amazingly – he managed to get the rest out of the country on elephants into India. All the other Columban priests in Myitkyina and Bhamo were imprisoned by now, but Jim, using all his rhetorical skills, had succeeded in persuading a Japanese commander, who had been educated in a Christian school in Tokyo, to leave him with the children. For his heroic rescue of these orphans, the Derry man was later awarded the MBE by the British government ('An official Member of the British empire! What will they say in Derry?' he joked), and while in India, he was recruited as an interpreter and adviser by Americans planning to drop intelligence gatherers behind Japanese lines.

Jim's tie with Kajihtu was now severed and Denis would remain there alone, although not unaffected by the encroaching war. The young boarders at Kajihtu went back to their villages, their families being fearful of both Japanese patrols and looting Chinese soldiers. The Kajhitans now looked to Denis as their protector. He had his refugee problem too, though military rather than civilian, which brings us to acting Captain Arthur Thompson, DSO, a desperate British soldier who figures as a kind of revenant, a surrogate brother, in Denis's life history.

23

Unlike Tom, Arthur Thompson was not a professional soldier. Neither his background nor his temperament could be said to have inclined him to soldiering. Orphaned at the age of eight, he was educated as a free boarder at Christ Hospital School in Sussex; his vacations were spent at the home of a parson friend of his parents who cared for him with well-remembered severity. At school, it was noted that he had a flair for English, but he was not academically inclined and excelled only at cricket.

So on completing his secondary education, he became a bank clerk, a role not unfitting for someone who would always say with emphasis that he was not a naturally brave man. After three years, however, the tedium of counting other men's money behind a counter weighed heavily upon him; he was almost relieved when in 1939, at the age of twenty-two, he found himself conscripted into the army, World War II having begun. Assigned to the Burma Rifles and soon commissioned, he anticipated an easy passage in a corner of the world that for him was no more than an exotic name, and where Hitler's ambitions posed no threats. But the case turned out to be otherwise: his Burma experience would prove exceptionally grim and give him a life-long preoccupation with the ways in which men behave when thrust unprepared into extreme situations. And in such situations he would surprise himself.

When the Japanese swept into Burma at the beginning of 1942, his experience, like that of the British army and the country's colonial administrators, was one of scrambling retreat and escape-if-you-can into India. On 23 March he was appointed temporary captain and given the task, with his company of 135 Karens, of delaying the advance of a whole battalion of Japanese infantry so that a detachment of Burma Levies could demolish a sequence of bridges on the road between Toungoo and Mawchi, a town near the border with Siam (Thailand) where most of the invading forces had been massed. Although outnumbered by about eight to one, and losing sixty-eight of his men, he inflicted heavy casualties on the enemy and completed his task successfully, showing – in the words of his DSO citation – 'The highest quality of courage, leadership, and skilful handling of his men throughout … His magnificent delaying action saved the Chinese and British armies in Burma from encirclement.' But this action was only the beginning of his Burma ordeal, and what lay ahead was all about endurance and judgment rather than combat. The bank clerk-turned-soldier emerges at the end more an Odysseus than an Achilles or a Hector (though he would never have encouraged such comparisons).

Towards the end of April, he and his sixty or so survivors found themselves bivouacked in the compound of a wooden government building in the riverside village of Mong Pawn, to the east of central Burma. They had been resting there for two days, enjoying the novelty of regular meals and sleeping off the effects of two months' continuous fighting. But Thompson was uneasy. His company had been left behind when all the other British forces switched to a north-westerly direction, heading for India across the Chindwin River at Kalewa; only the Chinese army remained in the south-east, holding the line a few miles from where he and his men were now resting. Then on the evening of 20 April, news came in that the Chinese lines had been broken and that the Japanese would very soon be arriving in strength. Orders or no orders, he had to move; he rightly anticipated a headlong rush by the enemy right up the eastern side of Burma as far as Myitkyina.

He had with him in his company of Karens a fellow Englishman and good friend, temporary captain Jimmy Nimmo, two experienced Karen NCOs, and two young Karen subalterns; on these he would rely greatly. Later they were joined by Captain King, a tin-miner who was with the RFC in World War I and had recently been drummed into the army. They all agreed with Thompson's suggestion that they should march north on the road to Lashio in the hope of getting transport and supplies there and perhaps joining a larger British unit that had not yet departed. After two days' marching, they were overtaken by a British brigadier driving towards Lashio; he stopped and told Thompson to take charge of a party of 150 men who were stranded further up the road without any officers. This was unwelcome news, the first of many shocks on his desperate journey: as well as his own, he now had to care for a party of inexperienced soldiers who would have to be fed and who would ultimately prove unreliable. Yet what lay ahead was far worse than he imagined at this stage. He was launched on a march with which the retreat from Mons to Paris was gentle by comparison.

24

The march of the expanded group began cheerfully enough, but they were soon attacked by Japanese dive-bombers. A busload of Chinese civilians disgorged behind them, and in seconds their wounded and dead were scattered about the road. Thompson and his men, however, managed to escape unharmed into the protection of paddy-field ditches. In the long trek north, which they were now beginning, enemy planes, enemy foot patrols, and the undisciplined remnants of a defeated Chinese army, who vied with them for food and shelter, became major obstacles to survival. For the present, they realized that the Japanese were likely to catch up with them on the Lashio road, so they decided to move across country and westwards to the town of Mamyo, still clutching the hope of finding transport to take them further north.

After three days' marching in extreme heat, many of them, including Thompson, were footsore and limping badly. Some were suffering from fever and all were exhausted and hungry, having been unable to purchase enough rice from the Shan villagers they encountered on the way. On the third day, they arrived at a village towards evening, only to find encamped on its outskirts about 350 bedraggled and hungry

Chinese soldiers who gave them resentful looks. Thompson, however, with the kind of foresight he would frequently display on this journey, had sent a runner ahead with money to bargain with the village headman for food, so that they were provided on arrival with enough for the night and the morrow. But he saw that the Chinese were heading in the same direction as themselves and recognized that from now on they would be in competition with these and perhaps other remnants of that broken army. He ensured that his own men rose and departed silently at dawn next morning, getting a head start on their rivals. They were now involved in a race within a race.

Good luck would often follow bad in this race (and vice versa). At the next village, they came upon a full battalion of Burma Rifles who were arranging to split up into three parties and take different routes north. They were very well-equipped, and their commander, Colonel Brocklehurst, was able to supply Thompson with rations, mules and muleteers, a pair of good canvas shoes to replace his own tattered specimens, and a substantial sum of money; this last would prove indispensable to their survival. Attached to the Battalion was a band of thirty commandos, led by a Captain Brown. The commandos' journey north would strangely criss-cross Thompson's; on each occasion their dwindling numbers and declining fortunes would be noted until the last few survivors of the group, deaf to the voice of wisdom and compassion, chose the wrong route and vanished forever in the swampy Hukawng Valley in the far north.

Thompson's first major test was on 1 May when he and his company arrived at a ferry point of the Nam Tu, a turbulent river 100 yards wide. Here they found a dangerous and chaotic situation. Three hundred of Brocklehurst's men and at least 1000 Chinese were already there, waiting to cross, their sole means of transport being one slender dugout canoe; clearly it would take many days to get everyone over. Thompson promptly formed a plan of his own and led his men further upriver until he found a position suited to his intention. Here he set some of them to making bamboo rafts, others to fit together from baggage ropes a line over 100 yards long, others to construct a jetty. These tasks were completed by midnight, and, in the grey glimmer of a misty dawn, the crossing was made. First the mules, led by a champion Karen swimmer, were sent over; the rope was secured on both sides and with difficulty lifted clear of the water; then it was used to assist the raft-crossings. Thompson, Jimmy and King were the last to cross, but not before Thompson had sent a message down to the Brocklehurst group offering them his ferry system, an exchange of baggage ropes facilitating the exercise. Thompson's leadership qualities and *esprit de corps* were becoming more and more apparent.

They marched for twelve hours and stopped for the night at a village where they learned to their dismay that the Japanese had already occupied Mamyo. They had covered 180 miles by now, and Thompson had been keeping up the spirits of the sick and the fainthearted by reiterating his promise of transport at Mamyo. Now, after some anguished reflection, he and Jimmy decided that their last hope of an assisted exit from the country lay in a swift, north-westerly march to Katha, southwest of Bhamo, where the British might still be holding a line. He called the men together, explained his thinking, and said they had to beat the Japanese to Katha; if not, it would mean attempting to walk all the way to the border with Assam in the far north, an attempt which few if any of them were likely to survive.

Exhausted and dispirited, they slept fitfully that night in the open under a clear starlit sky. Until well after midnight, the headlamps of Japanese lorries down below them swept through the treetops as they roared around and onwards in the direction of Mamyo. They left an ominous silence behind them. In his wakeful hours, Thompson found no solace in the remote splendours of the night sky; the winking stars seemed to mock his desperate plight.

25

For four days they marched in the intolerable heat that precedes the onset of the monsoon at the end of May, and across the most punishing terrain: an endless succession of hills. They knew that speed was essential, yet their pace was dictated by that of the sick; time and again they had to wait for the stragglers to catch up. Once they were overtaken by the commandos, the last time they would see that group together as a unit. Then they encountered and were jostled by a large party of Chinese who had taken possession of a little village and were casting envious eyes on their supplies. Fearful of being robbed, they branched off the track and had to cut their way through jungle.

Next day brought an extraordinary interlude, the kind to which war gives a unique intensity. It was a dreamlike experience of peacetime comfort and elegance as enjoyed by the Raj in the company of sophisticated and cooperative native princes; a fleeting perception of order and civility circumscribed by confusion and violence; a taste of British imperialism as it saw itself; a glimpse of *Pax Britannica*. Near a village in a pleasant valley, they came upon the Sawbwa of Momeik (Shan sawbwas were native princes who ruled over their provinces under the aegis of the British). This sawbwa was educated in England, had a charming English wife, and he and Thompson had met before in happier times. He and his wife and her Swiss companion were staying at his hunting lodge on the edge of a forest nearby, and although some two or three hundred evacuees from Momeik, bombed by the Japanese, were sheltering in his compound, the British officers and their men were given a generous welcome. The local villagers, said the Sawbwa, would arrange a special meal for the infantrymen, and the three British officers would dine and spend the night at the lodge, the Karen subalterns remaining with the privates and the NCOs.

There was dinner for six on the lawn. White cloth gleamed in brilliant moonlight on a great table, china and silver sparkled, glasses shone; Indian servants moved about with silent grace. The host and the ladies had dressed for dinner in the best colonial manner. At first, the three officers felt acutely embarrassed by their dishevelled and unshaven appearance, but the ladies were sympathetic and made light of it.

Conversation began pleasantly. Then anxieties came to the fore, for it was clear that the Japanese would be in Momeik in a day or two. Although the Sawbwa had a Bentley, a big Ford V8 and two lorries, he was not prepared to evacuate his family and abandon his people. But he was worried, having heard many unfavourable things about the Japanese; he was apprehensive too lest any accommodation he might make with these 'liberators' could be taken as disloyalty by the British on their hoped-for return.

Nevertheless, he had a plan for Thompson and his men to get to Katha. He suggested they could be ferried on his lorries up to Myitson on the River Shweli, one of the few large rivers in Burma to flow north; rafts could be built there by the first arrivals and then the company could float downriver to Ngao, which was close to Katha; the mules and muleteers would follow on foot. It would be no quicker than marching, but it would be far more comfortable, save a lot of energy and give them a much needed rest: their haggard looks had impressed him.

The plan worked. Arranging with the muleteers to meet them at Ngao, Thompson and his men moved off from Myitson the following morning and poled their way easily downstream. Congested though they were, they found it a pleasant experience, the extension of an interlude. At times they saw lines of Chinese soldiers and Indian and Gurkha refugees trudging along the right bank and blessed their own good fortune. Enemy planes flew northwards directly above them but this time showed no interest. In a strangely mournful style that was all their own, the Karens sang a range of songs learned at Baptist mission schools, among them 'She'll be Coming Round the Mountain' and 'John Brown's Body'. Always acutely sensitive to his natural environment, Thompson on the second night thrilled to the most wonderful sunset he had seen since coming to Burma: a vast redness eclipsed the western sky, enflamed the shimmering surface of the river, and made the dark forest seem darker still. They camped peacefully each night by quiet inlets.

26

Just before they reached Ngao, King lost his shoes overboard while bathing his battered feet; there was much laughter, especially among the Karens, but it was later seen as an ominous event, for at Ngao they were told that the Japanese had already taken Katha. Their hopes of transport finally shattered, they now had to face the prospect of walking, or trying to walk, every inch of the way to Assam. Acute disappointment verged dangerously on despair; Thompson concealed his feelings and concentrated minds on deciding which route to take. The shorter route was north-west across the plains; that, however, would expose them to Japanese reconnaissance and leave them reliant on the doubtful loyalties of the Burmese. The route east and then north through the jungly Kachin hills was longer and more difficult but undoubtedly safer; the friendliness of the Kachins, especially towards the British, was well-known. The three officers decided on the latter route and gave everyone else the option of either joining them, attempting a different route, or simply getting rid of their uniforms and melting back into their villages. Fifty of the Karen riflemen volunteered to join them, as did the muleteers; the rest were paid off and given as much of the rations as each could carry.

On the first day of the journey east, King's bare feet tormented him, as they would for a long time, and then something more ominous than his mishap on the river occurred. They were well into the hills when they came upon a lone British soldier lying beside the path. It was Private Lacey, one of the commandos who had by now broken up into four groups; he was so ill with dysentery that he had fallen behind his comrades and given up the struggle, resigned to a lonely death. Thompson and the others did not debate what should be done with him but propped him up on their pony; they resumed their journey in a distinctly gloomy state of mind, their silence punctuated from time to time by the hobbling King's muttered execrations. Thompson's and Jimmy's feet were not much better off; their shoes were wearing out, and every few miles they stuffed banana leaves into them, knowing, however, that they would soon disintegrate.

The monsoon started, and the rain came down in torrents. And their fortunes plunged when they awoke one morning to find that the muleteers had vanished, taking both the rations and the mules. From now on they were a collection of fifty hungry men dependent on what they could purchase from villagers and without animals to carry the sick. The time could come, each man thought, when he would have to tell his companions to leave him to face death alone. A few days later, a group of sturdy Gurkhas who joined them with the attachment near Pawn decided to strike out on their own; they saw failure written in the drawn faces and leaden steps of the British officers.

Thompson and his followers were now down to fourteen. This was good in a way, since they were a manageable group and all old comrades. But although they had a compass, they had no maps; they had covered an estimated 420 miles, their clothes torn and lousy with ticks, at least half of them now sick with malaria or dysentery or troubled by bruised or lacerated feet; they had no medicines. They were totally dependent on the Kachins for food and shelter and for guides through the hills. And they had 500 miles to go. They were extremely fortunate to have the rupees to pay for what they could get on the way, but they knew they would be very lucky if the money didn't run out before they reached India. Thompson became obsessed with the notion of Luck, both good and bad, and (as his son would reveal many years later) would remain so until his dying day.

27

They moved eastward for three days without food, existing on edible roots and water from the occasional stream. They arrived dazed and unsteady at their first Kachin village but were kindly received. They were given a huge meal of rice in banana leaves, with lots of rice wine, and then slept heavily in the space below the ground floor of the head-man's house. Next morning, they left with a guide and enough rice for a day or two. A strange fellow, this guide sang loudly and tunelessly all day long as he made his way up and down hills 1000 feet high and across gushing streams. Efficiently, he got them to another village just as dark-ness fell and blotted out everything. Rueful, Thompson thought: here is a man who knows exactly where he is going and how to get there.

Although friendly, the people in this village were extremely nervous and anxious for them to move on quickly: a Japanese patrol had paid them a visit, demanded food, taken two girls away ('comfort women'), and warned that harbouring or assisting the enemy would mean death. Again and again the soldiers would come upon villages that had been similarly treated and where they had difficulty in securing food and a night's rest. When allowed to spend the night in such villages, they slept with their equipment on, ready to shoot at a moment's notice. Outside the huts in many of the villages were pinned notices adorned with an image of the rising sun and promising rewards for the capture of British and Chinese soldiers – and death for all those who helped them; leaflets with this message had also been dropped from the air on some villages. On one occasion they heard the rattle of machine-gun fire and learned later that a group of Chinese who preceded them were ambushed by a Japanese patrol; they realized they had had a very narrow escape. But for the hatred that the Kachins had for both the Japanese and the Chinese (who roughly seized what food they could), the Kachins might never have given Thompson's company any assistance.

Still moving east, they had to cross the border into China before heading north. When Jimmy was extremely ill from malaria, they came upon a mission station that seemed heaven-sent. But it belonged to two priests, a Spaniard and an Italian, who were so fearful of Japanese patrols that they only allowed them to stay the night and bundled them out at dawn. Then they came to another mission station at the town of Maying. Here there was a French missionary, Father Lacoste, who behaved quite differently. He fed them well, treated Jimmy with some quinine, and let them rest at his place for several days. With painful honesty, he told them that although he had been here for several years, he was no great success as a missionary: 'Quite a number of the people here,' he told them, 'are Christians, but I am sure that if I were not sup-plied with some drugs and able to assist them in a practical way their Christianity would mean very little to them.'

Jimmy recovered, King purchased a crude pair of sandals, and they sold one rifle to a pestering Chinese headman who wanted all their guns. They moved north in the direction of Kachin territory, glad to be putting the unfriendly Chinese behind them. In a few days they came upon Fort Morton, a deserted British outpost, a kind of colonial ghost town. Inside its ancient battlemented walls were a barracks, a hospital, a post office and gun emplacements. They learned on the way that this fort had been occupied by an army detachment until quite recently and that the Japanese then came and looted everything of value. The place was a complete mess, littered with debris, eerily inhospitable. They climbed to the top of the battlements and through the swirling monsoon mists caught fleeting glimpses of jungle-covered hills surrounding them on all sides. They were daunted by the dereliction behind them and by an overpowering silence in those mists and hills. It seemed to mock every hope of survival: who were they to think they might escape through all of that?

Settling down for the night, they felt desperately helpless and alone; the inclination to despair was more threatening now than ever before. Morning brought no change of mood, but they decided to rest here for a few days. They had already exhausted every topic of conversation that might distract them from present woes, every fantasy feast and future, and every joke, so they spent their time playing cards, winning and losing huge imaginary sums. When reality became intolerable, imagination or hallucination took over.

28

It was mid-June when they left Fort Morton. The monsoon was in full swing, and the rain poured down in fierce leaden sheets that reduced their clothes to rags. The tracks were flooded, muddy and infested with leeches, the most unpleasant of all their jungle enemies. Quietly, insensibly, the leeches attacked every part of the body, gorging themselves with blood until they dropped off or were discovered. Especially in the rain, they could be almost impossible to detect; sometimes up to twenty of them, 1–3 inches long, could be attached to the body. Once every hour the men stopped to examine themselves from head to toe, removing them one by one with a bayonet or *dah*. The blood loss they caused accelerated debilitation; when the fang had not been extracted, the puncture produced infections of the foot.

On the first night after Fort Morton, they come upon a tumble-down government rest house where freshly opened fish tins, warning signs of the Japanese, are strewn about. They find a few unripe tomatoes growing nearby and devour them. Sent out to forage for food further afield, one of the Karens purchases a goat from some villagers; having no cooking utensils, they eat it raw, with ravenous satisfaction. Thompson reflects on how far they have come from their former lives, and wonders how much further they will sink; he has heard that some Chinese were reduced to eating the flesh of their dead companions. They move on in the morning.

All but one of them by now have had an attack of malaria, some of them twice. Their progress is very slow, even in those days when the sun breaks through for a few hours. Thompson is skeletal and his hip bones stick out, painful to any touch; he has no option now but to try sleeping on his face. It is an art, he says, that he will never acquire, but it is the only way he can rest. The bamboo floors of the villagers' huts hurt him terribly. Now, too, he has his worst attack of malaria, and to compound his misery his back is inflamed with a mass of boils. Sleepless for days, he staggers on as best he can and then collapses. So far, when one of the company was struck by malaria, he would lie by the track for twenty-four hours until he had sweated out the fever, and the others would sit down and wait until he could move on. But this time the effort to move on proves too much for him. After his twenty-four hours, the fever lifts, he trudges forward for a while behind the others, and then collapses. Feeling that he has exhausted every last ounce of strength and will, he insists that they leave him; when he feels better, he says (making his abandonment easier for them), he will follow them to the next village.

Reluctantly they move on without him, and he sees with grim clarity what lies in store for him. He is going to die beside the path as so many others have died in the past. His despair is total, not because of death, which now seems like a pleasant release, but because of the waiting. Surrounded by the evil jungle and the terrible silence of the hills, he will lie for days, not knowing how the end will come: by starvation pains or enteric fever, gnawed by a tiger or run through by a Japanese bayonet or a bounty-seeking tribesman.

He lies half-waking and half-sleeping for hours that seem years, then emerges from delirium at sunrise to the senseless chattering of monkeys high above and the squawking of some strange bird. Then silence again. His eye falls curiously on a spider's web glistening in the morning light; he stares fixedly at it as if it is the last thing he will ever see. He cannot connect that perfect design with the confusing mess into which his life has descended and is now ending. Time passes, he sleeps again and has a strange vision of himself as an insect, a speck, an atom, drifting up and beyond the indifferent stars into the black infinity of the unknown universe.

But he has not been abandoned, he is not nothing. Sitting cross-legged behind him, like some patient and compassionate Buddha, is Subedar-Major Kan Choke. An NCO of many years service, he was an inspiration during the fighting and now proves a great-hearted companion. The village, he tells the awakening Thompson, is perhaps five miles ahead, and they can make it. The prostrate captain pulls himself together enough to crawl forward on the narrow track, Kan Choke encouraging him. He manages between fifty and one hundred yards, rests for about five minutes, and then tries again. And again. His hands and knees become sore and torn, but as the hours go by he seems to recover some of his strength, and sometimes, if the track looks level, he gets up on his feet and totters a short distance with Kan Choke's help. It is the most ghastly day he has ever spent, and next morning he cannot remember how it ended; but he is told by the others that he joined them after dark and before falling asleep devoured a good meal they had saved for him. They feed him now with four eggs cooked in a bamboo container for four minutes. His energy returns sufficiently for them to move off, but from now on Jimmy effectively takes control of the party. Thompson knows how lucky he is to be still among the living. But it is not simply a matter of luck, he reflects: it lies in the nature of another human being – whom he was lucky to have in his company.

29

A few days later they learn at some village that the last remaining three or four of the commandos passed through a few days before; they were very sick, and Captain Brown, too ill with dysentery to move on, had been left behind (later they hear that he was captured by the Japanese). Two out of every three Kachin villages they pass through now are completely deserted or inhabited by a mere handful of men who have stayed behind as a sort of rearguard. Japanese patrols and scavenging Chinese have made the people so jittery that they have begun to take cover in the jungle. In these empty villages, the soldiers have no trouble finding shelter. But the silence is unnerving, their fear of the Japanese intense.

Some other villages they are anxious to pass through as silently and quickly as possible. From time to time they come across dead or dying Chinese soldiers lying by the trackside, and sometimes they overtake walking skeletons who stare at them in hopeless silence: all victims of dysentery, malaria, cholera, beri-beri, starvation. Then one beautiful moonlit night, when the air is sweet and cool after the heat of the day, and they are profoundly weary after their long march, they round a bend and find themselves on the outskirts of a village, a cluster of huts both large and small, silent and apparently deserted. As they advance they are overcome by a powerful stench; Thompson's stomach heaves, and he almost vomits. Holding his nose he approaches the first of the huts. The foul smell has seeped through its bamboo walls. He looks inside and sees that the place is littered with Chinese corpses, blackened and swollen. Every hut is the same, but not all the shapes are dead. Some groan when they see him; one body raises a bony arm feebly in the gloom. The dead and the dying lie side by side in the stinking shadows. Horrified, Thompson clambers down the rickety steps as fast as his shaky legs will carry him.

They have had no food now for two days and are driven to eat raw snake and a slimy soup made of jungle leaves and roots boiled in bamboo. They get water from a cool mountain stream and fill their bottles from it. But before moving on, they get down on all fours to bathe their flushed and dirty faces in the stream. As he raises his face from the water, Thompson is appalled to see the swollen body of a Chinese soldier lying in the water hardly ten yards upstream, partly concealed by overhanging branches. For days afterwards they fear the worst and later marvel how they escaped a death-dealing contamination.

30

Their hope is now to cross the Nmai, north of Myitkyina, into the Triangle. Once over it and into the hills on the far side, they could head north in the direction of Fort Hertz; they know it has an airstrip and think it might still be used by the British. Luck favours them when Jimmy questions a young Kachin whom they come across fishing near his village. He used to work for a British engineer in Lashio, and when his master was captured he escaped and made his way home; he now volunteers to lead them to the Nmai Haka – and for nothing. He transfers to them his feeling for the lost master who treated him well.

Towards midnight they reach Sadon, a village that lies directly in their path. They are exhausted, but their guide tells them that the Japanese left it recently and that there are spies in it – Burmese, presumably: it is no place to stay. Cautiously, he enters the village alone to reconnoitre and then returns to lead them through in complete silence. Here and there a light twinkles, and the scent of burning wood hangs in the air; a twig snaps underfoot, a dog barks; in single file, stealthily, they pass through unchallenged. They advance into a profound darkness intermittently broken by the odd firefly.

By about three in the morning, they drop down into a shallow valley where the paddy fields are deep with water and the mud on the track reaches above their ankles. Their guide points to a glimmer of light ahead. It comes from a lonely cultivator's hut in the middle of a paddy; it is to be their resting place for the night. Wading out to it, they try not to arrive any more wet and muddy than they already are, but the soft mud underfoot is treacherous and few of them arrive without having fallen down. 'Shit, shit!' mutters King, dragging himself up. 'I volunteered for the Flying Corps in 1916 just to get away from this sort of thing. Now I'm back in the army and the mud. Oh fly, fly, fly!' Not for the first time, he remembers the dangerous ecstatic freedom of soaring and swooping in the skies above Belgium and France in his flimsy Sopwith Camel. Knowing that the end, if it came, would be quick and clean..

Reaching the hut, they climb up a bamboo ladder and crowd into a small space already occupied by an opium-sodden cultivator and his son. Seemingly indifferent to their presence, the two move over and allow the visitors to lie down side by side – warmly wet, filthy and longing for sleep.

They reach the Nmai two days later, and it terrifies them. It's about 200 yards wide, and its waters, swollen by the recent heavy rains, are in seething turmoil. It goes roaring past them, great clumps of driftwood bobbing upon its surface, white foam dancing around rocks that obstruct its furious onrush. The local village headman secures a raft for them. It is shallow and loosely strung together and compares very badly with the raft made by the Karens at the Nam Tu; they look at it in dismay. 'It's suicide to try crossing in that,' says Jimmy quietly to Thompson. But they are desperate: 400 yards behind them, running parallel to the river, is the Myitkyina–Hpimaw road, currently being used by the Japanese; that fact outweighs Thompson's initial judgment that they should wait until the river calms down. The attempt is duly made and nearly ends in complete disaster. The raft soon spins out of control, and one of the two Kachin polers loses his pole and panics. Then it crashes against a large flat rock far from where they started; it falls apart, and while the others scramble on to the rock Thompson misses his hold and is about to be swept away when someone grabs his arm and helps him up. They cling to the rock for three hours and then are immensely relieved to see that the Karens on shore have kept following them down. The Karens form a human chain connected by bamboo poles and slowly bring the bedraggled survivors back to dry land, one by one. But Thompson has lost his compass in the swirling waters; he wonders if it means that all along he was fated to go nowhere. The daily menace of death has made him superstitious.

They spend a tense and miserable week waiting for the river to quieten, hiding in a lean-to thrown together for them by the villagers. They feed on wild figs growing plentifully nearby and are sold some rice by the villagers. Too tired and depressed to talk or play cards, they are constantly worried by the sound of Japanese lorries going up and down the road, and intensely fearful when news is brought to them that twenty Japanese soldiers are in the village. But the soldiers leave the next day, the river gradually subsides, and on 1 July a successful crossing is made: this time on a much better-constructed raft, prudently carrying two and not six men per crossing as before. 'As you live you learn,' says Thompson. 'If you're lucky to live.'

31

The group feel somewhat safer in the Triangle. But the going is extremely tough, and it begins to seem very doubtful whether their health – Thompson's in particular – will enable them to go much further. The monsoon rains are still relentless and the tracks so muddy and overgrown that progress is desperately slow. They get badly scratched and the low-lying ground seems an especially fertile place for the breeding of leeches: never before have they encountered so many. The usual hourly halt to scrape them off is replaced by one every fifteen minutes; blood loss increases, fatigue is overwhelming. The villages they reach each night are the most unsanitary they have ever encountered, and some nights they are so tormented by mosquitoes that they abandon all attempts to sleep and instead huddle round the fire until dawn. Three of the Karens have malarial attacks. Then on the fifth night, Thompson's right foot begins to ache unbearably, and when morning comes he is unable to put it on the ground. It is hugely swollen and inflamed, an infection gifted to him by the leeches and the filth. Gloomily he remembers hearing that one of the commandos had to be left behind because he was similarly affected. The faithful Kan Choke, however, although himself unwell, will not leave him; he has a rough stretcher made and manages to find half a dozen wild-looking men to act as paid carriers.

This arrangement seems worthwhile, for they have heard that some days' march away there is a village with a mission station where rest and medical help might be found; but could that be a cruel rumour? Seemingly more promising news arrives on the following night when a half-naked Kachin armed with a spear comes into the headman's hut where they are staying and tells them in pidgin Burmese that 'the Government has come back. In umbrellas. Yesterday evening in Ningchangyang.'

True or false, news that parachutists have landed has an electrifying effect upon everyone, however weary and sick. Here, they sense, is tangible contact with the army in India, a feeling of escape as a real possibility rather than a forlorn dream, a feeling too that something more positive than helter-skelter retreat on the part of the British is going on. In Burmese, they quizz the newsbearer repeatedly to make sure that the parachutists are not Japanese and to find out how they are equipped and in what strength they have come. That night they talk excitedly among themselves – Ningchangyang is only about three miles away. Very unusually, they are awake long after their native hosts.

Impatient to catch up with the parachutists, Jimmy Nimmo goes off next morning with the others, leaving Kan Choke to supervise the carrying of Thompson. It is an agonizing experience for the invalid. The path wends sharply down a vertiginous hillside around numerous hairpin bends, and it takes several hours to reach the plain below. The carriers slip and fall, Thompson's hip bones compel him to lie on his chest, and his foot, huge and shiny-red, throbs as if it will burst. Yet the thought of those parachutists makes the pain easier to bear. And when they reach the bottom, they move along smoothly at a fair pace.

Nanchingyang turns out to be quite a big village surrounded by extensive paddy fields. But it seems worryingly quiet. Perhaps, he wonders, the parachutists were Japanese after all, perhaps Jimmy and the others have been taken? He tells the others to pause and look around. Then an old man pops his head out of a hut; he informs them that the soldiers from the sky are staying at a government rest house – a large bamboo affair with a few other huts beside it – half a mile further on.

And there, amazingly, they are, chatting with Jimmy on the verandah. Holding on to Kan Choke, Thompson hobbles forward to shake hands with them. They are white-skinned and clean-shaven, their shirts and shorts still crisp from their last laundering. He is suddenly conscious of his own dreadful appearance: gaunt, bearded, filthy. There are twelve parachutists in all: Captain Roberts, a sergeant major, two wireless operators and eight Gurkhas. Their mission is to find out about an airfield in the Myitkyina area, to discover how far the Japanese have moved from Myitkyina towards Fort Hertz, and to report on the local population's reaction to the Japanese. Their mission accomplished, they intend to make their way to Fort Hertz, which is still not occupied by the Japanese, patch up its pitted airstrip, and wait to be picked up and flown out to Assam. None of them speak Burmese, however, so two of their Gurkhas dressed as Kachins have been sent off to Myitkyina to contact the local Indians there, but the Gurkhas return on the following day, having been unable to cross the Mali River. Like the Hka, it was in full flow, and Japanese soldiers were visible on the far side.

Jimmy and Thompson act as badly needed informants and translators for Roberts, telling him of the Kachins' fear and hatred of the Japanese, assuring him that he will find them natural allies; he recruits two of them to undertake the Myitkyina mission. Roberts is stunned to learn that in the last three months Thompson's group has walked an estimated 730 miles; and when Thompson looks aghast at the position of Fort Hertz on the newcomers' map, Roberts quips: 'A mere 250 miles more should be no problem for you chaps.' Thompson does not appreciate the joke. In his present condition, how could he manage that? His elation begins to seep away; temporarily suspended by all this excitement, pain and exhaustion return.

It is decided that Jimmy should stay with Roberts as translator. King and the others will push on to the mission village, and Thompson will try to catch up with them when (and if) his foot improves. Then when the Kachins return from Myitkyina, Roberts and Jimmy will follow. But Thompson's group has been fed for three whole days by Roberts, and he feels guilty about lingering on and draining the parachutists' rations even more; thus he decides he should leave if at all possible. Despite bathing his foot in potassium permanganate, it is no better, so the day after King's departure he gets Kan Choke to scour Nanchinyang for a horse. He is away all afternoon and returns before sundown. Wearily, he squats down beside Thompson:

'I have got a horse for you, *thakin* [sir]. But it is skinny and sick. Skinnier than you are, *thakin*.'

'Can it walk?'

'Yes, it can walk.'

'Okay. We're off tomorrow.'

It is duly brought to the rest house by its owner, who bargains irritatingly for much more than he gets in the end. It is a sad specimen, blind in one eye, its great bones protruding through its dull hide. 'My double,' says Thompson glumly.

He has great difficulty keeping his swollen foot in the stirrup, and when they have gone only four miles and reached the village of Mara, he decides he has had enough for the day. Kan Choke's condition too deteriorates, and with it Thompson's flickering optimism gives way once more. But they find lodgings with the village headman, and Thompson has his first experience of native medicine. The headman seems very perturbed about the foot. He props it up on his knee, gives it a thorough examination, and then pronounces that he can cure it. Sceptical and wary, Thompson politely declines the offer, but Kan Choke persuades him to change his mind: at least no harm can come of it, he argues, failing to hide his conviction that there is no hope for Thompson otherwise; he knows how quickly the killer gangrene can set in.

A strange concoction is brewed from leaves and plants of all kind, a hot poultice is applied, and the doctoring headman declares that about midnight the foot will hurt badly for five or six hours, then it will start to improve. He is right. The burning sensation is so bad that the patient is barely restrained by Kan Choke from tearing off the 'vegetation' (as he calls it), but when it is removed in the morning and the green sediment washed off, the inflammation is considerably reduced. A delighted Thompson finds that he is now able to hobble about.

Mounted on his miserable nag, with the faithful Kan Choke plodding beside him and with his paid guide out in front, he is able to cover eight miles that day. He has a reasonable night's rest in an abandoned hut, and next day they set off very early: he is impatient to reach the mission, of whose existence he has recently been assured, to rest and get well again and to rejoin the others. But the bony nag obstinately refuses to move; it seems to know, as animals do, that its end has come. After much cajoling and loss of time, Thompson decides to leave it behind. His foot is much better but is still painful, and his pace cannot match his eagerness; it takes all day to cover eight miles and cross the Tara, a minor stream about thirty yards wide. In late afternoon on the next day, they come to a clearing in the plain, and their guide points upwards.

In his memoir, *Desperate Journey*, written two years later and published under the pseudonym Francis Clifford, Thompson says: 'We could see it alright, perched up like the mythical Shangri-La at the top of a mist-enshrouded hill.' (*Desperate Journey* [London: Hodder and Stoughton 1979], p. 147.) It is Kajihtu, the village that coincides with an unnamed dot to the east of Sumprabum on Roberts's map. Kan Choke is eager to get to it before sundown, but Thompson feels he has exhausted his last ounce of energy and insists that they will have to wait until sunrise. They find a deserted hut further down the valley, and after a frugal meal of rice and jungle leaves they fall asleep. That night Thompson has his first pleasant dream in three months; so far his dreams have all been feverish and distressing. This one is a recurring but rare dream he has had since childhood, one which happens when his mood of the day has been especially confident or joyous: in it he spreads his arms out as if they are wings, soars high above houses and fields, above trees and entangling telegraph poles, and is saying to himself even in his dream, 'I really can fly, this is not a dream, I am in control.'

Arthur Thompson before and after his ordeal. Courtesy of Mr Peter Thompson.

Before setting off next morning they hear, as they have heard for several days now, aircraft going over from west to east; they can't see them but they know from the familiar drone that they are Allied planes on the milk run between India and Chiang Kai Chek's army in China; they give a tantalizing feeling of nearness to 'home' even though the border is at least 200 miles away.

Leaning heavily on his bamboo stick, Thompson climbs slowly and painfully up the hill, Kan Choke helping when he stumbles. Every fifteen minutes he sits down to rest his foot and recover his breath. He is grateful for the morning mist that cools his face. Two hours later they emerge from the jungle on to the top of the hill. The mists have evaporated and in the sunlit clearing before them everything stands out in crisp outline, as if to say that this is no dream:

> The village was right in front of us, dominated by the mission house and one or two adjacent buildings. King spotted us from the verandah and came running down the steep wooden steps to greet us. It was good to see him again ... but his face was horribly shrunken and his handshake feeble. He led us inside and introduced us to Father McAlindon, a clean-shaven, soft-spoken Irishman, on the right side of forty. He was a charming fellow and we were friends from the start.
>
> The first thing he did was to give us a terrific breakfast of pancakes and jam, which we disposed of with scant ceremony.
>
> (*Desperate Journey*, p. 148.)

Thompson is surprised to find that they are not the only refugees at the mission. The three remaining members of Brown's commandos are also there and have been for over three weeks: 'bearded, hollow-eyed strangers, unrecognisable from the men we had last seen near the Si-u road'. These men are ready and impatient to move on again.

That night he sleeps in a room next to the little chapel in the mission house. He wakes in the morning to the sound of Father Denis's voice, audible through the thin wall, starting to say Mass in a pleasant, comforting monotone; murmuring in the language that brought the material and then the spiritual power of Rome to the remotest corners of the earth: '*Introibo ad altare Dei, ad Deum qui laetificat iuventutem meum.*' ('I will go in unto the altar of God, unto God who giveth joy to my youth.')

'Joy cometh in the morning,' Thompson recalls from somewhere in the Bible. He lies quietly for a while on the two bedrolls Denis has given him, then rises and goes out to the verandah. He looks up and sees it is going to be a fine day; he remembers those Hudsons high in the sky and his own aerial dream.

But Father Denis is troubled. Before breakfast he tells Thompson that the commandos intend to travel down into the Hukawng Valley and that he has tried in vain to change their minds. Trackless and for the most part under water, it has been a death trap for thousands of refugees; everybody knows it is impassable. But the commandos obstinately maintain that Fort Hertz must have been taken by now by the Japanese and that Hukawng offers the only hope of escape. Denis told them that a runner had been sent down to Father Stuart in Sumprabum and would soon bring back news as to the whereabouts of the Japanese and that they should wait until his return. But they have been in Kajihtu for three weeks and are impatient to leave. Although their departure would ease the demands on Denis's stores, he asks Thompson to see if he can dissuade them.

Thompson goes into the other room and argues with them for about an hour, but they are immovable. They say they are fed up hanging around, that they have found a guide and are ready to go. Resignedly, he shakes hands with them and bids them good luck. From the edge of the village he watches them follow their guide unsteadily down the hill.

They are never heard of again: three desperate British soldiers whom Denis's best efforts could not save. His distress after their departure is visible to everyone. They do not know that he is remembering the worst day of his life.

The two Karen subalterns in Thompson's group, Ba Gyaw and Saw Tory, had already succumbed to malaria when Thompson arrived, but now Kan Choke catches it, too, as does Thompson yet again. And to cap it all, King has a recurrence of his dysentery. Denis gives the malarial victims daily doses from his store of quinine, King he treats successfully with the new sulpha drug. When they are feeling better, he manages to give them one sound meal each day.

Besides medication, rest and companionship, there are books to read. Although Thompson finds it hard to concentrate for any length of time, reading is a welcome escape from the dragging hours and the nagging uncertainty of his future. One of the two books he reads is John Buchan's *Greenmantle*, a classic adventure tale about a dauntless soldier-turned-spy. Curiously, Denis's copy of that same book will find its way back with his other few possessions to Derryloiste some six years later, where it will be read with enthusiasm by two of his nephews during their summer holidays. More importantly, the novel plants in Thompson's mind an idea of what he might do with himself as an alternative to bank-clerking if and when he survives this war.

He reached Kajihtu around 13 July and leaves after two weeks. He tries to leave earlier, feeling guilty about the extent to which they are depleting the priest's stores of medicine and tinned food. But Denis delays their departure, saying they are not strong enough yet to face the last leg of their journey. They agree to leave a week later although even by then the runner from Sumprabum has not come through; but just as they are about to set out a British plane flies low over the mission several times, banking slightly from side to side, signalling awareness of some kind. It is clearly on the lookout for Roberts's party, whose wireless was damaged in their descent and with whom contact from base was lost. (A week later, the airmen learn from Denis, by way of dropped messages on their part and simple signals on his, that Roberts has passed through and is on his way to Fort Hertz.)

Such is their excitement on seeing this plane, and construing it as a good augury for the future, that they delay their parting until the next day. They talk late and sleep fitfully but are up at dawn. At breakfast they are quiet, for they don't find it easy to say goodbye to their generous and kindly host (*Desperate Journey*, p. 153). Realizing how he has exposed himself to the wrath of the Japanese, they have already urged him to come with them to Fort Hertz and thence to India, but he refused, saying simply, 'My place is here. We priests can do little enough in peacetime, and now that the Kachins want our help it is essential not to desert them.' Now they try again to persuade him, but to no avail. (Except for a quick expedition into India to secure medicines and supplies from the Americans, he stays in Kajihtu until recalled in 1947.) Resigned to his refusal, and fearful for his future at the hands of the Japanese, they say goodbye, led by the guide he has found for them. He follows them for a short distance down the steep track, and then stands waving until they pass over the next hill and they can see him no more.

In his memoir, Thompson writes that at that moment he felt he would never forget Denis, and he did not. But he never did know that Denis saw in his emaciated face, and in the faces of his fellow soldiers, the face of his brother Tom. The saving of Thompson and his friends filled a void, healed a wound that was in Denis's heart since he was eleven years old. Strange and yet not strange that Thompson should have felt that they were 'friends from the start'.

On 24 August, after some tormenting delays and postponements at Fort Hertz, due mainly to the condition of the airstrip, Thompson and his men, with Roberts and the other parachutists, are flown out to Assam. As the plane pulls ponderously away and then levels out on a western course, he sees the Himalayas in all their white magnificence dominating the northern sky, and then the green mountains below beginning to slide past them. He is overcome by feelings of exhilaration and incredulity: 'We are out! We are out!' he cries, and those words keep running through his head. But then words that more adequately express his feelings come to mind as he remembers a poem written when World War I finally ended – two months after Tom's death – by Captain Siegfried Sassoon, MC, a famous survivor of the Western Front:

> Everyone suddenly burst out singing;
> And I was filled with such delight
> As prisoned birds must find in freedom,
> Winging wildly across the white
> Orchards and dark green fields; on; and on; and out of sight ...
> (Quoted in *Desperate Journey*, p. 188.)

32

Thompson was invalided back to England in late 1942: his weight had dropped from twelve to eight stone, his health was poor even after several months in hospital. During his convalescence at home he wrote *Desperate Journey* in an attempt to exorcize his Burmese demons. After the War, he returned to Civvy Street, taking a job as a publicity writer in London for a large manufacturing firm. He also married his childhood sweetheart, by whom he had a daughter and a son.

But his Burmese nightmare had made it impossible for him to settle down to civilian routine, and in the 1950s he began writing fiction, concentrating on novels of suspense and adventure in which he could explore character, especially when placed in dangerous situations. Under the pseudonym of Francis Clifford, he wrote twenty novels, all published by Hodder and Stoughton, publishers of John Buchan's *Greenmantle*. World sales of his books passed the five million mark. They were translated into fifteen languages; three of them were filmed and he was twice awarded the Crime Writers' Association Silver Dagger Award and twice the Mystery Writers of America's Edgar Allen Poe Award. A reviewer in *The Times Literary Supplement* said of him that 'he writes from a deep understanding of violence born of his own experiences but also

– and this is his main strength – from compassion and a sensitivity to despair'. *The Guardian* described him as 'unique in combining deeply felt philosophical truth with the excitement of a thriller'. 'The thinking man's Ian Fleming' was how one reviewer described him. To the surprise of many, he also became a Catholic.

Strangely, *Desperate Journey* was not published (as by Francis Clifford, but with an explanatory introduction by a friend) until 1979, four years after his death. This long delay, I suspect, is connected with the nature of his first novel, *Honour the Shrine* (London: Hodder and Stoughton 1953), in which a British officer, Captain Strachan, is dropped behind Japanese lines in Burma one year after the great retreat, his mission being to blow up a key bridge. The success of this mission is entirely dependent on the help given him by an Irish missionary priest who risks and loses his life in order to do so, being subsequently beheaded by the Japanese for aiding the enemy. His mission accomplished, Strachan urges the priest to leave with him on the plane that flies in to pick him up and is incredulous when he says: 'I would never quit Samprulam ... My work is here, with these people; to desert them now would be shameful.' Thus Strachan leaves the priest to go

> back to the loneliness, the privation, the scanty monotonous food, the ever-present threat of Japanese action ... bringing God to a handful of converts and a sense of security to everyone within the area, tending their wounds and sickness, tramping the hills from village to village, conserving his dwindling stores, encouraging and advising ... And the Brigadier would say, 'How damned extraordinary!'
> (*Honour the Shrine*, pp. 127, 167.)

Denis returned on leave to Ireland in 1948 and in 1949 was sent back to Burma as the Society's vice-pro-director there, being based in Bhamo. He returned to Ireland again in 1952 when he was elected vicar general of the Society, an office to which he was re-elected in 1962. He is still remembered by some old priests in the Society for the wisdom, gentleness and good humour that he exercised in that capacity. Among his other duties he had to do much travelling in an advisory capacity to the Society's missions in widely different parts of the world; and this he greatly enjoyed. He was efficient and conscientious in the performance of his administrative responsibilities, but I doubt if he greatly enjoyed them. He died in 1993, aged eighty-seven.

A singularly modest and reticent man, he never told anyone in the family about his dangerous times in Kajihtu. A year before he died, however, my friend Alex Ashe sent me a photocopy of the ten pages in *Dangerous Journey* dealing with Kajihtu, and on my next visit home I quizzed Denis about 'Francis Clifford', whose real name I did not know at the time – I would only learn it two years later when I came across a copy of the out-of-print book, where it is revealed in the introduction written by Thompson's friend. Denis had a superb memory, which he retained to the end, and seemed cross with himself for being unable to remember a 'Captain Clifford'; when he abandoned the effort, he added by way of excuse and (typically) without elaboration, 'But there were so many.'

The implications of that give-away remark were further revealed to me recently when I consulted the archives of the Society and found in Denis's file an extraordinary letter dated 30 May 1964, written by one Daniel Mudrinich of Fairfax, Virginia. It was written on behalf of the 101 Detachment Association of the US army, the fledgling OSS (Office of Strategic Services, forerunner of the CIA), whose members regularly parachuted into Burma after 1942 on intelligence and subversion missions (for an account of their derring-do activities, with the aid of Kachin guerrillas, see www.burmastar.org.uk/101stair.htm). The writer invited Denis to attend a 101 Association Reunion, assuring him that air travel and all other expenses would be paid for:

> Your contribution to our war effort in Burma, which was manifested in so many ways, is not easily expressed. The months that I spent with you are still vivid in my memory and I recall special little incidents which have shaped my outlook on life and my feelings towards my

fellow man. Your patience, humility, and extremely wise judgement have left an impression on all of us and perhaps have made us better men than we would be had we never met you.

I would guess that Denis replied in the kindest terms that he would love to attend but that his present responsibilities made it impossible for him to do so. Collective adulation would have embarrassed him. Father Jim Stuart did receive such adulation from the Americans and took it easily in his stride: his exploits featured in a long article in *Collier's Magazine* and he was met by Hollywood notabilities (including the director John Ford and the actor Pat O'Brien) on his arrival in Los Angeles, where he was to receive an honour. At the end of the War an OSS agent asked Jim to write a report of his experiences, which he did. In the final paragraph he said:

> Father McAlindon had a more exciting time than I had but he was not so fortunate in his publicity agents. Colonel Eifler [the first member and commander of Detachment 101] once confided to me that at the beginning the OSS didn't want me at all. They wanted Father Mac but they took me to be sure of getting Father Mac. Later he said that – well, I had a certain publicity value [the MBE?]. You should ask Father Mac to give you some facts of his life during the war years, for publicity purposes. I don't think you will succeed, but at any rate you will get a lesson in real humility to counteract this egotistical report of mine. (Quoted in Edward Fischer, *Mission in Burma* [New York: Seabury Press 1986], pp. 69–70.)

After his retirement in the late 1970s Denis did not reside, as most of his retired confreres did, in the Society's gracious house in Dalgan Park, County Meath. Instead, he returned to the cottage in Derryloiste where he was born, helping out in a number of country parishes in that area, renewing his contacts with all the families he grew up with, liking nothing better than to drop in for a fireside chat where he was always a welcome guest; in short, living a life not entirely unlike his life in Kajihtu. In Derryloiste too he was near to his beloved Eddie and Mary Ellen, who lived in Belfast, and to their children and grandchildren, in whose company he delighted. He died in 1993, aged eighty-seven.

One of my sisters, who often chaffed him in a way that none of the rest of us would have dared, suggested to him a few years before he died that he should never have become a priest but should have been a doctor or an academic and got married and had a family. Always somewhat enigmatic, guarding his inner self, he laughed and changed the subject and she never knew whether he meant, 'You could be right' or, 'You would never understand.' He was meticulous in the performance of his priestly duties, and maintained a perfect correctness of clerical behaviour humanized by a natural courtesy and an ironic good humour. But in conversation I never once heard him mention God or utter a pious sentiment. That may have been a part of his reticence, but I often wondered if he saw his achievements in life as humane and moral rather than theological and spiritual; I have to wonder too if he could have done so much good for others had he not been a missionary priest.

On something else, however, he was very clear. In the course of a long conversation about our family history during my last visit to him I happened to ask him what he remembered as the best part of his long life. I thought he might say the years of global travelling as vicar general, or his postgraduate years in Rome when as a young man and priest he beheld on a daily basis the splendours of the Eternal City – St Peter's with its daunting magnificence, more modest San Clemente with its multi-layered history, Michelangelo and all that classical statuary too. But no. Without a moment's reflection he replied (and his tone indicated that there could be no other answer): 'Oh, Burma.'

Which, of course, meant Kajihtu, where his ghost of Tom was laid to rest.

SOURCES AND SELECT BIBLIOGRAPHY

Archival Sources

Gill, Father H., War Reminiscences, 1914–1918, Irish Jesuit
     Archives, Dublin.
McAlindon, Thomas, Regimental Record, National Archives,
     Kew, 339/103552.
War Diary of the 2nd Battalion of the Royal Irish Rifles, National
     Archives, Kew, WO95/1415, WO95/2247 and WO95/2502.

Selected Secondary Sources

Brown, Malcolm, *The Imperial War Museum Book of the Western Front*,
     revd. edn (London: Pan Books 2001).
Burgoyne, Gerald Achilles, *The Burgoyne Diaries* (London:
     Harmsworth 1985).
Clifford, Francis (aka Arthur Thompson), *Honour the Shrine* (London:
     Hodder and Stoughton 1953).
——, *Desperate Journey* (London: Hodder and Stoughton 1979).
Falls, Cyril, *The History of the First Seven Battalions: The Royal Irish Rifles
     (now the Royal Ulster Rifles) in the Great War* (Aldershot: Gale and
     Polden 1925).

Fischer, Edward, *Mission in Burma* (New York: Seabury Press 1986).

Laffin, John, *On the Western Front* (Sutton: Stroud 1985).

Laurie, Lt. Col. G.B., *History of the Royal Irish Rifles* (London: Gale and Polden 1914).

Lucy, John, *There's a Devil in the Drum* (East Sussex: The Naval and Military Press 1938).

McAlindon, Denis, 'Fr Jim Stuart: a great missionary', *The Far East*, November 1955, 7–15.

Taylor, James W., *The 2nd Royal Irish Rifles* (Dublin: Four Courts Press 2005).